THE SCHOLAR'S LIBRARY
General Editor :—GUY BOAS, M.A.

POEMS OLD AND NEW
AN ANTHOLOGY

POEMS OLD AND NEW
AN ANTHOLOGY

Selected and Edited by
A. S. CAIRNCROSS
M.A., D.LITT.

MACMILLAN AND CO., LIMITED
ST. MARTIN'S STREET, LONDON

COPYRIGHT

First Edition 1933
Reprinted September and December 1934, *June a:*

PRINTED IN GREAT BRITAIN
BY R. & R. CLARK, LIMITED, EDINB

ACKNOWLEDGMENTS

THE compiler wishes to acknowledge his indebtedness to the following for permission to reprint the copyright poems included in this volume: Mr. Stephen Vincent Benét and Messrs. Doubleday, Doran & Co. for "Portrait of a Boy" from *Young Adventure*; Mr. Edmund Blunden and Messrs. Sidgwick & Jackson, Ltd., for "The Pike" from *The Waggoner*; the Literary Executor and Messrs. Sidgwick & Jackson, Ltd., for "The Dead," by Rupert Brooke; Messrs. Chatto & Windus for "The Vagabond" and "Romance," by Robert Louis Stevenson; Mr. G. K. Chesterton and Messrs. J. M. Dent & Sons, Ltd., for "The Donkey"; the Clarendon Press for "A Passer-by" from *The Poetical Works of Robert Bridges*; Mr. Walter de la Mare for "Tit for Tat" and "I met at Eve"; the author's Executors and Messrs. Martin Secker, Ltd., for "The Old Ships" from *Collected Poems*, by James Elroy Flecker; Mr. W. W. Gibson for "Prometheus" from *Collected Poems 1905-1925*; Captain Harry Graham and Messrs. Edward Arnold & Co., Ltd., for "Waste" from *Ruthless Rhymes*; Messrs. William Heinemann, Ltd., for "Itylus," by Algernon Charles Swinburne; Mr. Ralph Hodgson for "Stupidity Street" from his *Poems*; the Owners of the Copyright for "Pied Beauty," by Gerard Manley Hopkins; Messrs. John Lane, The Bodley Head, Ltd., for "The Hawk," by A. C. Benson; Mr. John Masefield for "Cargoes" from *Collected Poems by John Masefield* (Heinemann); Messrs. Methuen & Co., Ltd., for "Jack" from *The Open Road*, by Mr. E. V. Lucas; Mr. John Murray for "Hervé Riel," by Robert Browning; Sir Henry Newbolt for "Hawke," "He Fell Among Thieves," and "Drake's Drum" from *Poems New and Old* (John Murray); Mr. Alfred Noyes and Messrs. William Blackwood & Sons, Ltd., for "The Highwayman" from *The Collected Poems of Alfred Noyes*; the Poetry Bookshop for "Star Talk" from *Over the Brazier*, by Mr. Robert Graves, and "The Changeling" from *The Farmer's Bride*, by Charlotte Mew; the Proprietors of *Punch* for "Roundabouts and Swings," by Mr. P. R. Chalmers; Mr. Grant Richards for "A Runnable Stag" from *Holiday and Other Poems*, by John Davidson; Mr. Siegfried Sassoon and Messrs. William Heinemann, Ltd., for "Everyone Sang"; Sir John Squire and Messrs. William Heinemann, Ltd., for "The Ship" from *Poems in One Volume*; Sir William Watson for "The Ballad of Semmerwater"; and Mr. W. B. Yeats for "The Lake Isle of Innisfree" from *Poems* (Ernest Benn), and "The Scholars" from *The Wild Swans at Coole*.

CONTENTS

BALLADS

		PAGE
Sir Patrick Spens	*Anonymous*	3
Helen of Kirconnell	*Anonymous*	6
Rosabelle	*Sir Walter Scott*	7
Proud Maisie	,,	8
Bishop Hatto	*Robert Southey*	9
La Belle Dame sans Merci	*John Keats*	12
The Knight's Leap	*Charles Kingsley*	13
Horatius	*Lord Macaulay*	15
Shameful Death	*William Morris*	24
The Ballad of Semmerwater	*Sir William Watson*	25

NARRATIVE POEMS

Hart-Leap Well	*William Wordsworth*	29
The Destruction of Sennacherib	*Lord Byron*	35
The Armada	*Lord Macaulay*	36
Morte d'Arthur	*Lord Tennyson*	40
The Lady of Shalott	,,	47
Hervé Riel	*Robert Browning*	53
The Pied Piper of Hamelin	,,	58
Goblin Market	*Christina Rossetti*	67
A Runnable Stag	*John Davidson*	83
Hawke	*Sir Henry Newbolt*	86
He Fell Among Thieves	,,	87
The Highwayman	*Alfred Noyes*	89

vii

CONTENTS

LYRICAL AND DESCRIPTIVE POEMS

		PAGE
The Passionate Shepherd to his Love	Christopher Marlowe	97
Winter	William Shakespeare	98
Fidele	,,	98
Character of a Happy Life	Sir Henry Wotton	99
To Celia	Ben Jonson	100
Hymn to Diana	,,	101
The Village Preacher *and* Schoolmaster (from *The Deserted Village*)	Oliver Goldsmith	101
The Tiger	William Blake	104
The Solitary Reaper	William Wordsworth	105
Upon Westminster Bridge	,,	106
She Dwelt Among the Untrodden Ways	,,	106
Lullaby of an Infant Chief	Sir Walter Scott	107
Soldier, rest !	,,	107
Coronach	,,	109
Pibroch of Donuil Dhu	,,	109
Kubla Khan	Samuel Taylor Coleridge	111
The Parrot	Thomas Campbell	112
She Walks in Beauty	Lord Byron	113
To Night	Percy Bysshe Shelley	114
The Human Seasons	John Keats	115
On first looking into Chapman's Homer	,,	116
To Autumn	,,	117
Autumn	John Clare	118
The Eagle	Lord Tennyson	119
Blow, Bugle, blow	,,	119
Home-thoughts, from Abroad	Robert Browning	120
O Captain ! my Captain !	Walt Whitman	120

CONTENTS

		PAGE
The Scholar Gipsy	Matthew Arnold	121
Itylus	A. C. Swinburne	130
Pied Beauty	Gerard Manley Hopkins	132
A Passer-by	Robert Bridges	133
The Vagabond	R. L. Stevenson	134
Romance	,,	135
Drake's Drum	Sir Henry Newbolt	135
The Hawk	A. C. Benson	136
The Lake Isle of Innisfree	W. B. Yeats	137
The Scholars	,,	137
Jack	E. V. Lucas	138
The Changeling	Charlotte Mew	142
Stupidity Street	Ralph Hodgson	144
Roundabouts and Swings	Patrick R. Chalmers	145
Tit for Tat	Walter de la Mare	146
I met at Eve	,,	147
The Donkey	G. K. Chesterton	148
Cargoes	John Masefield	149
Prometheus	Wilfrid Gibson	149
The Ship	Sir John Squire	150
The Old Ships	James Elroy Flecker	150
Everyone Sang	Siegfried Sassoon	151
The Dead	Rupert Brooke	152
The Pike	Edmund Blunden	152
Portrait of a Boy	Stephen Vincent Benét	154

WIT AND HUMOUR

Sir Hudibras and his Squire (from *Hudibras*)	Samuel Butler	157
The Character of Shaftesbury (from *Absalom and Achitophel*)	John Dryden	159
Epitaph on Charles II	Earl of Rochester	159

CONTENTS

		PAGE
The Combat (from *The Rape of the Lock*)	Alexander Pope	160
On a certain Lady at Court	,,	162
Elegy on the Death of a Mad Dog	*Oliver Goldsmith*	163
Fred	*Anonymous*	164
The Colubriad	*William Cowper*	164
The desired Swan-Song	*Samuel Taylor Coleridge*	166
The Jackdaw of Rheims	*R. H. Barham*	166
King Canute	*W. M. Thackeray*	171
You are old, Father William	*Lewis Carroll*	174
Waste	*Harry Graham*	175
Star Talk	*Robert Graves*	176
Notes to the Poems		179
Questions on the Poems		217

INTRODUCTION

For some chosen spirits a love of poetry comes and grows of itself. They pass without effort from the early delight in nursery rhymes to the works of the great poets ; their natural interest is strong enough to brush aside all obstacles that stand between them and the pleasures of poetry.

But for others—and these are the majority—a taste for poetry must be carefully tended and fostered. Taste is for most of us a matter of slow growth and continuous study and training. It cannot be formed without knowledge, comparison, and analysis of the best poetry : and this cannot be acquired without assistance and guidance. A thorough acquaintance, gained in this way, with even a few great poems, is a sufficient foundation for a sound and lasting delight. These few poems, however, must be treated naturally. They must be read aloud, since poetry is meant to appeal to the ear. They should be read, and read again, and, best of all, committed to memory. The sense of the poem and the intention of the poet should be made perfectly clear, and any information that will serve this end should be brought to bear. A new light is often shed on a poem by some fact concerning the author, the age in which he lived, or the circumstances in which he wrote.

Goldsmith's simple nature, Macaulay's retentive memory, Keats's ill-health, Pope's deformity, Flecker's life in the East, lay bare the springs and direction of

INTRODUCTION

their poetry as a whole, and make its excellencies and its limits intelligible. Without a knowledge of Dryden's dependence on court patronage and of the political and religious struggle over the Exclusion Bill, it is impossible fully to appreciate his satires, especially *Absalom and Achitophel*. The dream in which Coleridge composed *Kubla Khan* and the interruption which prevented him from remembering the whole poem, the description that inspired Wordsworth's *Solitary Reaper*, explain much that would otherwise be obscure, and effectively heighten our appreciation. To understand is to forgive : it is also to appreciate.

It is often illuminating, too, if a comparison is made between poems by two authors on the same theme, or between a poem and the source on which it is founded. To compare Tennyson's *Morte d'Arthur* with the original prose version of Malory is a valuable lesson in criticism and appreciation : to read Marlowe's *Passionate Shepherd to his Love* along with Stevenson's *Romance*, Wotton's *Happy Life* or W. B. Yeats's *Lake Isle of Innisfree* is to throw into relief the characteristic qualities of each poet. But the main thing is the poetry itself, and criticism and commentary are justified only in so far as they add to the enjoyment of the poetry : they must never be allowed to usurp the main interest.

On such a foundation of reading, understanding, and memory, good taste and appreciation may be trusted to rise of themselves. A touchstone will have been provided to which other poems may be brought for judgment : a core will have been formed round which will gather other poems that have been tried and found worthy.

This anthology aims at providing material for the formation of a sound poetic appreciation. While avoiding more difficult and abstract poems, it con-

INTRODUCTION

tains a representative selection of the best in English poetry—not omitting that of the present day. It supplies explanatory material and suggestions for comparison and criticism that may remove difficulties and clear the way for that delight in poetry which is one of the most valuable and lasting acquisitions in life.

For the characteristic of good poetry is that the enjoyment of it is unfailing. It was a poet who wrote " A thing of beauty is a joy for ever," and of no thing is this more true than of a beautiful poem.

A. S. C.

BALLADS

SIR PATRICK SPENS

1. *The Sailing*

The king sits in Dunfermline town
   Drinking the blude-red wine ;
" O whare will I get a skeely skipper
   To sail this new ship o' mine ? "

O up and spak an eldern knight,
   Sat at the king's right knee ;
" Sir Patrick Spens is the best sailor
   That ever sail'd the sea."

Our king has written a braid letter,
   And seal'd it with his hand,   10
And sent it to Sir Patrick Spens,
   Was walking on the strand.

" To Noroway, to Noroway,
   To Noroway o'er the faem ;
The king's daughter o' Noroway,
   'Tis thou must bring her hame."

The first word that Sir Patrick read
   So loud, loud laugh'd he ;
The neist word that Sir Patrick read
   The tear blinded his e'e.   20

" O wha is this has done this deed
    And tauld the king o' me,
To send us out, at this time o' year,
    To sail upon the sea ?

" Be it wind, be it weet, be it hail, be it sleet,
    Our ship must sail the faem ;
The king's daughter o' Noroway,
    'Tis we must fetch her hame."

They hoysed their sails on Monenday morn
    Wi' a' the speed they may ;   10
They hae landed in Noroway
    Upon a Wodensday.

II. *The Return*

" Mak ready, mak ready, my merry men a' !
    Our gude ship sails the morn."
" Now ever alack, my master dear,
    I fear a deadly storm.

" I saw the new moon late yestreen
    Wi' the auld moon in her arm ;
And if we gang to sea, master,
    I fear we'll come to harm."   20

They hadna sail'd a league, a league,
    A league but barely three,
When the lift grew dark, and the wind blew loud,
    And gurly grew the sea.

The ankers brak, and the topmast lap,
    It was sic a deadly storm :
And the waves cam owre the broken ship
    Till a' her sides were torn.

SIR PATRICK SPENS

" Go fetch a web o' the silken claith,
    Another o' the twine,
And wap them into our ship's side,
    And let nae the sea come in."

They fetch'd a web o' the silken claith,
    Another o' the twine,
And they wapp'd them round that gude ship's side,
    But still the sea came in.

O laith, laith were our gude Scots lords
    To wet their cork-heel'd shoon ;   10
But lang or a' the play was play'd
    They wat their hats aboon.

And mony was the feather bed
    That flatter'd on the faem ;
And mony was the gude lord's son
    That never mair cam hame.

O lang, lang may the ladies sit,
    Wi' their fans into their hand,
Before they see Sir Patrick Spens
    Come sailing to the strand !   20

And lang, lang may the maidens sit
    Wi' their gowd kames in their hair,
A-waiting for their ain dear loves !
    For them they'll see nae mair.

Half-owre, half-owre to Aberdour,
    'Tis fifty fathoms deep ;
And there lies gude Sir Patrick Spens,
    Wi' the Scots lords at his feet !
                               ANONYMOUS

POEMS OLD AND NEW

HELEN OF KIRCONNELL

I WISH I were where Helen lies,
Night and day on me she cries ;
O that I were where Helen lies,
   On fair Kirconnell lea !

Curst be the heart that thought the thought,
And curst the hand that fired the shot,
When in my arms burd Helen dropt,
   And died to succour me !

O think na ye my heart was sair,
When my Love dropp'd and spak nae mair ! 10
There did she swoon wi' meikle care,
   On fair Kirconnell lea.

As I went down the water-side,
None but my foe to be my guide,
None but my foe to be my guide,
   On fair Kirconnell lea ;

I lighted down my sword to draw,
I hackèd him in pieces sma',
I hackèd him in pieces sma',
   For her sake that died for me. 20

O Helen fair, beyond compare !
I'll mak a garland o' thy hair,
Shall bind my heart for evermair,
   Until the day I die !

I wish I were where Helen lies !
Night and day on me she cries ;
And I am weary of the skies,
   For her sake that died for me.
                       ANONYMOUS

ROSABELLE

O LISTEN, listen, ladies gay !
  No haughty feat of arms I tell ;
Soft is the note, and sad the lay,
  That mourns the lovely Rosabelle.—

" Moor, moor the barge, ye gallant crew !
  And, gentle ladye, deign to stay !
Rest thee in Castle Ravensheuch,
  Nor tempt the stormy firth to-day.

" The blackening wave is edged with white ;
  To inch and rock the sea-mews fly ;   10
The fishers have heard the Water-Sprite,
  Whose screams forebode that wreck is nigh.

" Last night the gifted Seer did view
  A wet shroud swathed round ladye gay ;
Then stay thee, Fair, in Ravensheuch :
  Why cross the gloomy firth to-day ? "—

" 'Tis not because Lord Lindesay's heir
  To-night at Roslin leads the ball,
But that my ladye-mother there
  Sits lonely in her castle-hall.   20

" 'Tis not because the ring they ride,
  And Lindesay at the ring rides well,
But that my sire the wine will chide
  If 'tis not fill'd by Rosabelle."—

O'er Roslin all that dreary night
  A wondrous blaze was seen to gleam ;
'Twas broader than the watch-fire's light,
  And redder than the bright moonbeam.

POEMS OLD AND NEW

It glared on Roslin's castled rock,
  It ruddied all the copse-wood glen ;
'Twas seen from Dryden's groves of oak,
  And seen from cavern'd Hawthornden.

Seem'd all on fire that chapel proud,
  Where Roslin's chiefs uncoffin'd lie,
Each Baron, for a sable shroud,
  Sheath'd in his iron panoply.

Seem'd all on fire within, around,
  Deep sacristy and altar's pale ;   10
Shone every pillar foliage-bound,
  And glimmer'd all the dead men's mail.

Blazed battlement and pinnet high,
  Blazed every rose-carved buttress fair—
So still they blaze, when fate is nigh
  The lordly line of high St. Clair.

There are twenty of Roslin's barons bold
  Lie buried within that proud chapelle ;
Each one the holy vault doth hold—
  But the sea holds lovely Rosabelle !   20

And each St. Clair was buried there,
  With candle, with book, and with knell ;
But the sea-caves rung, and the wild winds sung,
  The dirge of lovely Rosabelle.

SIR WALTER SCOTT

PROUD MAISIE

PROUD Maisie is in the wood,
  Walking so early ;
Sweet Robin sits on the bush,
  Singing so rarely.

BISHOP HATTO

" Tell me, thou bonny bird,
    When shall I marry me ? "
" —When six braw gentlemen
    Kirkward shall carry ye."

" Who makes the bridal bed,
    Birdie, say truly ? "
" —The grey-headed sexton
    That delves the grave duly.

" The glow-worm o'er grave and stone
    Shall light thee steady ;   10
The owl from the steeple sing
    Welcome, proud lady ! "
              Sir Walter Scott

BISHOP HATTO

The summer and the autumn had been so wet
That in winter the corn was growing yet ;
'Twas a piteous sight to see all around
The grain lie rotten on the ground.

Every day the starving poor
Crowded around Bishop Hatto's door,
For he had a plentiful last-year's store,
And all the neighbourhood could tell   20
His granaries were furnish'd well.

At last Bishop Hatto appointed a day
To quiet the poor without delay ;
He bade them to his great barn repair,
And they should have food for the winter there.

Rejoiced such tidings good to hear,
The poor folk flock'd from far and near ;
The great barn was full as it could hold
Of women and children, and young and old.

POEMS OLD AND NEW

Then when he saw it could hold no more,
Bishop Hatto he made fast the door,
And while for mercy on Christ they call,
He set fire to the barn and burnt them all.

" I' faith, 'tis an excellent bonfire ! " quoth he,
" And the country is greatly obliged to me,
For ridding it in these times forlorn
Of rats, that only consume the corn."

So then to his palace returned he,
And he sat down to supper merrily,   10
And he slept that night like an innocent man.
But Bishop Hatto never slept again.

In the morning as he enter'd the hall,
Where his picture hung against the wall,
A death-like sweat all over him came ;
For the rats had eaten it out of the frame.

As he look'd there came a man from the farm,
He had a countenance white with alarm ;
" My lord, I open'd your granaries this morn,
And the rats had eaten all your corn."   20

Another came running presently,
And he was pale as pale could be ;
" Fly ! my Lord Bishop, fly," quoth he,
" Ten thousand rats are coming this way—
The Lord forgive you for yesterday ! "

" I'll go to my tower on the Rhine," replied he ;
" 'Tis the safest place in Germany ;
The walls are high, and the shores are steep,
And the stream is strong, and the water deep."

BISHOP HATTO

Bishop Hatto fearfully hasten'd away,
And he cross'd the Rhine without delay,
And reach'd his tower, and barr'd with care
All the windows, doors, and loopholes there.

He laid him down and closed his eyes,
But soon a scream made him arise ;
He started, and saw two eyes of flame
On his pillow from whence the screaming came.

He listen'd and look'd ; it was only the cat ;
But the Bishop he grew more fearful for that, 10
For she sat screaming, mad with fear,
At the army of rats that was drawing near.

For they have swum over the river so deep,
And they have climb'd the shores so steep,
And up the tower their way is bent,
To do the work for which they were sent.

They are not to be told by the dozen or score ;
By thousands they come, and by myriads and more ;
Such numbers had never been heard of before,
Such a judgment had never been witness'd of yore. 20

Down on his knees the Bishop fell,
And faster and faster his beads did he tell,
As louder and louder drawing near
The gnawing of their teeth he could hear.

And in at the windows, and in at the door,
And through the walls helter-skelter they pour,
And down from the ceiling, and up through the floor,
From the right and the left, from behind and before,
From within and without, from above and below,
And all at once to the Bishop they go. 30

They have whetted their teeth against the stones,
And now they pick the Bishop's bones ;
They gnaw'd the flesh from every limb,
For they were sent to do judgment on him.
                    ROBERT SOUTHEY

LA BELLE DAME SANS MERCI

" Oh what can ail thee, knight-at-arms,
    Alone and palely loitering ?
The sedge is wither'd from the lake,
    And no birds sing.

" Oh, what can ail thee, knight-at-arms,
    So haggard and so woebegone ?
The squirrel's granary is full,
    And the harvest's done.

" I see a lily on thy brow
    With anguish moist and fever dew ;
And on thy cheek a fading rose
    Fast withereth too."

" I met a lady in the meads,
    Full beautiful—a faery's child ;
Her hair was long, her foot was light,
    And her eyes were wild.

" I made a garland for her head,
    And bracelets too, and fragrant zone ;
She look'd at me as she did love,
    And made sweet moan.

" I set her on my pacing steed
    And nothing else saw all day long,
For sideways would she lean, and sing
    A faery's song.

THE KNIGHT'S LEAP

" She found me roots of relish sweet,
  And honey wild and manna dew,
And sure in language strange she said,
  ' I love thee true ! '

" She took me to her elfin grot,
  And there she wept, and sigh'd full sore ;
And there I shut her wild, wild eyes
  With kisses four.

" And there she lullèd me asleep,
  And there I dream'd—Ah ! woe betide ! 10
The latest dream I ever dream'd
  On the cold hill's side.

" I saw pale kings and princes too,
  Pale warriors, death-pale were they all ;
Who cried—' La belle Dame sans Merci
  Hath thee in thrall ! '

" I saw their starved lips in the gloam
  With horrid warning gapèd wide,
And I awoke and found me here
  On the cold hill's side.   20

" And this is why I sojourn here
  Alone and palely loitering,
Though the sedge is wither'd from the lake,
  And no birds sing."
                              JOHN KEATS

THE KNIGHT'S LEAP

" So the foemen have fired the gate, men of mine ;
  And the water is spent and gone ?
Then bring me a cup of the red Ahr-wine :
  I never shall drink but this one.

POEMS OLD AND NEW

" And reach me my harness, and saddle my horse
    And lead him me round to the door :
He must take such a leap to-night perforce,
    As horse never took before.

" I have fought my fight, I have lived my life,
    I have drunk my share of wine ;
From Trier to Cöln there was never a knight
    Led a merrier life than mine.

" I have lived by the saddle for years two score,
    And if I must die on tree,   10
Then the old saddle-tree, which has borne me of yore,
    Is the properest timber for me.

" So now to show bishop, and burgher, and priest,
    How the Altenahr hawk can die :
If they smoke the old falcon out of his nest,
    He must take to his wings and fly."

He harnessed himself by the clear moonshine,
    And he mounted his horse at the door ;
And he drained such a cup of the red Ahr-wine,
    As man never drained before.   20

He spurred the old horse, and he held him tight,
    And he leapt him out over the wall—
Out over the cliff, out into the night,
    Three hundred feet of fall.

They found him next morning below in the glen,
    With never a bone in him whole—
A mass or a prayer now, good gentlemen,
    For such a bold rider's soul !
                    CHARLES KINGSLEY

HORATIUS

They held a council standing
  Before the River-Gate ;
Short time was there, ye well may guess,
  For musing or debate.
Out spake the Consul roundly :
  " The bridge must straight go down ;
For, since Janiculum is lost,
  Nought else can save the town."

Just then a scout came flying,
  All wild with haste and fear :
" To arms ! to arms ! Sir Consul :
  Lars Porsena is here."
On the low hills to westward
  The Consul fixed his eye,
And saw the swarthy storm of dust
  Rise fast along the sky.

And nearer fast and nearer
  Doth the red whirlwind come ;
And louder still and still more loud,
From underneath that rolling cloud,
Is heard the trumpet's war-note proud,
  The trampling, and the hum.
And plainly and more plainly
  Now through the gloom appears,
Far to left and far to right,
In broken gleams of dark-blue light,
The long array of helmets bright,
  The long array of spears.

But the Consul's brow was sad,
  And the Consul's speech was low,
And darkly looked he at the wall,
  And darkly at the foe.

POEMS OLD AND NEW

"Their van will be upon us
  Before the bridge goes down;
And if they once may win the bridge,
  What hope to save the town?"

Then out spake brave Horatius,
  The Captain of the Gate:
"To every man upon this earth
  Death cometh soon or late.
And how can man die better
  Than facing fearful odds,
For the ashes of his fathers,
  And the temples of his Gods?"

"Hew down the bridge, Sir Consul,
  With all the speed ye may;
I, with two more to help me,
  Will hold the foe in play.
In yon strait path a thousand
  May well be stopped by three.
Now who will stand on either hand,
  And keep the bridge with me?"

Then out spake Spurius Lartius;
  A Ramnian proud was he:
"Lo, I will stand at thy right hand,
  And keep the bridge with thee."
And out spake strong Herminius;
  Of Titian blood was he:
"I will abide on thy left side,
  And keep the bridge with thee."

"Horatius," quoth the Consul,
  "As thou sayest, so let it be."
And straight against that great array
  Forth went the dauntless Three.

HORATIUS

For Romans in Rome's quarrel
  Spared neither land nor gold,
Nor son nor wife, nor limb nor life,
  In the brave days of old.

Now while the Three were tightening
  Their harness on their backs,
The Consul was the foremost man
  To take in hand an axe :
And Fathers mixed with Commons
  Seized hatchet, bar, and crow,   10
And smote upon the planks above
  And loosed the props below.

Meanwhile the Tuscan army,
  Right glorious to behold,
Came flashing back the noonday light,
Rank behind rank, like surges bright
  Of a broad sea of gold.
Four hundred trumpets sounded
  A peal of warlike glee,
As that great host with measured tread, 20
And spears advanced, and ensigns spread,
Rolled slowly towards the bridge's head,
  Where stood the dauntless Three.

The Three stood calm and silent,
  And looked upon the foes,
And a great shout of laughter
  From all the vanguard rose :
And forth three chiefs came spurring
  Before that deep array ;
To earth they sprang, their swords they 30
    drew,
And lifted high their shields and flew
  To win the narrow way.

POEMS OLD AND NEW

Stout Lartius hurled down Aunus
  Into the stream beneath ;
Herminius struck at Seius,
  And clove him to the teeth :
At Picus brave Horatius
  Darted one fiery thrust ;
And the proud Umbrian's gilded arms
  Clashed in the bloody dust.

But now no sound of laughter
  Was heard among the foes,
A wild and wrathful clamour
  From all the vanguard rose.
Six spears' lengths from the entrance
  Halted that deep array,
And for a space no man came forth
  To win the narrow way.

But hark ! the cry is " Astur ! "
  And lo ! the ranks divide ;
And the great Lord of Luna
  Comes with his stately stride.
Upon his ample shoulders
  Clangs loud the fourfold shield,
And in his hand he shakes the brand
  Which none but he can wield.

He smiled on those bold Romans
  A smile serene and high ;
He eyed the flinching Tuscans,
  And scorn was in his eye.
Quoth he, " The she-wolf's litter
  Stands savagely at bay :
But will ye dare to follow,
  If Astur clears the way ? "

HORATIUS

Then, whirling up his broadsword
  With both hands to the height,
He rushed against Horatius,
  And smote with all his might.
With shield and blade Horatius
  Right deftly turned the blow.
The blow, though turned, came yet too nigh ;
It missed his helm, but gashed his thigh :
The Tuscans raised a joyful cry
  To see the red blood flow.   10

He reeled, and on Herminius
  He leaned one breathing-space ;
Then, like a wild cat mad with wounds,
  Sprang right at Astur's face.
Through teeth, and skull, and helmet,
  So fierce a thrust he sped,
The good sword stood a hand-breadth out
  Behind the Tuscan's head.

And the great Lord of Luna
  Fell at that deadly stroke,   20
As falls on Mount Alvernus
  A thunder-smitten oak.
Far o'er the crashing forest,
  The giant arms lie spread ;
And the pale augurs, muttering low,
  Gaze on the blasted head.

On Astur's throat Horatius
  Right firmly pressed his heel,
And thrice and four times tugged amain,
  Ere he wrenched out the steel.   30
" And see," he cried, " the welcome,
  Fair guests, that waits you here !
What noble Lucumo comes next
  To taste our Roman cheer ? "

POEMS OLD AND NEW

But at his haughty challenge
  A sullen murmur ran,
Mingled of wrath, and shame, and dread,
  Along that glittering van.
There lacked not men of prowess,
  Nor men of lordly race ;
For all Etruria's noblest
  Were round the fatal place.

But all Etruria's noblest
  Felt their hearts sink to see   10
On the earth the bloody corpses,
  In the path the dauntless Three :
And, from the ghastly entrance,
  Where those bold Romans stood,
All shrank, like boys who unaware,
Ranging the woods to start a hare,
Come to the mouth of the dark lair
Where, growling low, a fierce old bear
  Lies amidst bones and blood.

Was none who would be foremost   20
  To lead such dire attack :
But those behind cried " Forward ! "
  And those before cried " Back ! "
And backward now and forward
  Wavers the deep array :
And on the tossing sea of steel,
To and fro the standards reel ;
And the victorious trumpet-peal
  Dies fitfully away.

But meanwhile axe and lever   30
  Have manfully been plied ;
And now the bridge hangs tottering
  Above the boiling tide.

20

HORATIUS

" Come back, come back, Horatius ! "
  Loud cried the Fathers all.
" Back, Lartius ! back, Herminius !
  Back, ere the ruin fall ! "

Back darted Spurius Lartius ;
  Herminius darted back :
And, as they passed, beneath their feet
  They felt the timbers crack.
But when they turned their faces,
  And on the farther shore   10
Saw brave Horatius stand alone,
  They would have crossed once more.

But with a crash like thunder
  Fell every loosened beam,
And, like a dam, the mighty wreck
  Lay right athwart the stream :
And a long shout of triumph
  Rose from the walls of Rome,
As to the highest turret-tops
  Was splashed the yellow foam.   20

And, like a horse unbroken
  When first he feels the rein,
The furious river struggled hard,
  And tossed his tawny mane,
And burst the curb, and bounded,
  Rejoicing to be free,
And whirling down, in fierce career,
  Battlement, and plank, and pier,
    Rushed headlong to the sea.

Alone stood brave Horatius,   30
  But constant still in mind ;
Thrice thirty thousand foes before,
  And the broad flood behind.

POEMS OLD AND NEW

" Down with him ! " cried false Sextus,
   With a smile on his pale face.
" Now yield thee," cried Lars Porsena,
   " Now yield thee to our grace."

Round turned he, as not deigning
   Those craven ranks to see ;
Nought spake he to Lars Porsena,
   To Sextus nought spake he :
But he saw on Palatinus
   The white porch of his home ;
And he spake to the noble river
   That rolls by the towers of Rome.

" Oh, Tiber ! father Tiber !
   To whom the Romans pray,
A Roman's life, a Roman's arms,
   Take thou in charge this day ! "
So he spake, and speaking sheathed
   The good sword by his side,
And with his harness on his back
   Plunged headlong in the tide.

No sound of joy or sorrow
   Was heard from either bank ;
But friends and foes in dumb surprise,
With parted lips and straining eyes,
   Stood gazing where he sank ;
And when above the surges
   They saw his crest appear,
All Rome sent forth a rapturous cry,
And even the ranks of Tuscany
   Could scarce forbear to cheer.

But fiercely ran the current,
   Swollen high by months of rain :
And fast his blood was flowing ;
   And he was sore in pain,

HORATIUS

And heavy with his armour,
  And spent with changing blows :
And oft they thought him sinking,
  But still again he rose.

Never, I ween, did swimmer,
  In such an evil case,
Struggle through such a raging flood
  Safe to the landing-place ;
But his limbs were borne up bravely
  By the brave heart within,   10
And our good father Tiber
  Bare bravely up his chin.

" Curse on him ! " quoth false Sextus ;
  " Will not the villain drown ?
But for this stay, ere close of day
  We should have sacked the town ! "
" Heaven help him ! " quoth Lars Porsena,
  " And bring him safe to shore ;
For such a gallant feat of arms
  Was never seen before."   20

And now he feels the bottom ;
  Now on dry earth he stands ;
Now round him throng the Fathers
  To press his gory hands ;
And now, with shouts and clapping,
  And noise of weeping loud,
He enters through the River-Gate,
  Borne by the joyous crowd.

And still his name sounds stirring
  Unto the men of Rome,   30
As the trumpet-blast that cries to them
  To charge the Volscian home ;

23

POEMS OLD AND NEW

And wives still pray to Juno
  For boys with hearts as bold
As his who kept the bridge so well
  In the brave days of old.
                    LORD MACAULAY

SHAMEFUL DEATH

THERE were four of us about that bed ;
  The mass-priest knelt at the side,
I and his mother stood at the head,
  Over his feet lay the bride ;
We were quite sure that he was dead,
  Though his eyes were open wide.   10

He did not die in the night,
  He did not die in the day,
But in the morning twilight
  His spirit pass'd away,
When neither sun nor moon was bright,
  And the trees were merely grey.

He was not slain with the sword,
  Knight's axe, or the knightly spear,
Yet spoke he never a word
  After he came in here ;   20
I cut away the cord
  From the neck of my brother dear.

He did not strike one blow,
  For the recreants came behind,
In a place where the hornbeams grow,
  A path right hard to find,
For the hornbeam boughs swing so,
  That the twilight makes it blind.

THE BALLAD OF SEMMERWATER

They lighted a great torch then,
   When his arms were pinion'd fast,
Sir John the knight of the Fen,
   Sir Guy of the Dolorous Blast,
With knights threescore and ten,
   Hung brave Lord Hugh at last.

I am threescore and ten,
   And my hair is all turn'd grey,
But I met Sir John of the Fen
   Long ago on a summer day,   10
And am glad to think of the moment when
   I took his life away.

I am threescore and ten,
   And my strength is mostly pass'd,
But long ago I and my men,
   When the sky was overcast,
And the smoke roll'd over the reeds of the fen,
   Slew Guy of the Dolorous Blast.

And now, knights all of you,
   I pray you pray for Sir Hugh,   20
A good knight and a true,
   And for Alice, his wife, pray too.
                     WILLIAM MORRIS

THE BALLAD OF SEMMERWATER

NORTH-COUNTRY LEGEND

Deep asleep, deep asleep,
   Deep asleep it lies,
The still lake of Semmerwater
   Under the still skies.

And many a fathom, many a fathom,
  Many a fathom below,
In a king's tower and a queen's bower
  The fishes come and go.

Once there stood by Semmerwater
  A mickle town and tall ;
King's tower and queen's bower,
  And the wakeman on the wall.

Came a beggar halt and sore :
  " I faint for lack of bread."
King's tower and queen's bower
  Cast him forth unfed.

He knocked at the door of the herdman's cot,
  The herdman's cot in the dale.
They gave him of their oatcake,
  They gave him of their ale.

He has cursed aloud that city proud,
  He has cursed it in its pride ;
He has cursed it into Semmerwater
  Down the brant hillside ;
He has cursed it into Semmerwater,
  There to bide.

King's tower and queen's bower,
  And a mickle town and tall ;
By glimmer of scale and gleam of fin,
  Folk have seen them all.

King's tower and queen's bower,
  And weed and reed in the gloom ;
And a lost city in Semmerwater,
  Deep asleep till Doom.

SIR WILLIAM WATSON

NARRATIVE POEMS

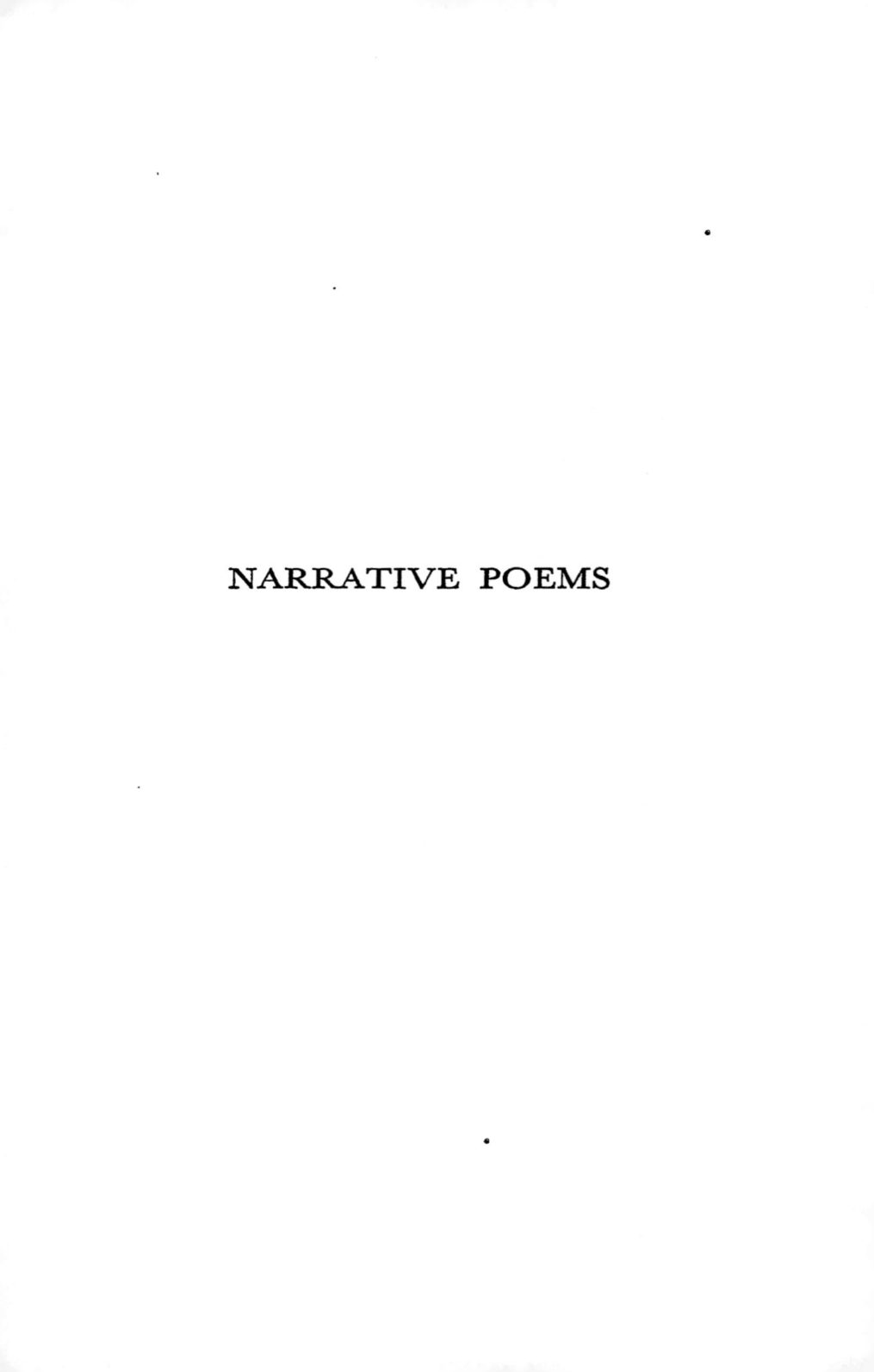

HART-LEAP WELL

Knight had ridden down from Wensley Moor
h the slow motion of a summer's cloud,
now, as he approached a vassal's door,
ing forth another horse ! " he cried aloud.

nother horse ! "—That shout the vassal heard
l saddled his best steed, a comely grey ;
Walter mounted him ; he was the third
ich he had mounted on that glorious day.

sparkled in the prancing courser's eyes ;
horse and horseman are a happy pair ; 10
, though Sir Walter like a falcon flies,
re is a doleful silence in the air.

out this morning left Sir Walter's hall,
it as they galloped made the echoes roar ;
horse and man are vanished, one and all ;
h race, I think, was never seen before.

Walter, restless as a veering wind,
ls to the few tired dogs that yet remain :
nch, Swift, and Music, noblest of their kind,
low, and up the weary mountain strain. 20

Knight hallooed, he cheered and chid them on
h suppliant gestures and upbraidings stern ;
breath and eyesight fail ; and, one by one,
dogs are stretched among the mountain fern.

Where is the throng, the tumult of the race?
The bugles that so joyfully were blown?
—This chase it looks not like an earthly chase;
Sir Walter and the hart are left alone.

The poor hart toils along the mountain-side;
I will not stop to tell how far he fled,
Nor will I mention by what death he died;
But now the Knight beholds him lying dead.

Dismounting, then, he leaned against a thorn;
He had no follower, dog, nor man, nor boy: 10
He neither cracked his whip, nor blew his horn,
But gazed upon the spoil with silent joy.

Close to the thorn on which Sir Walter leaned
Stood his dumb partner in this glorious feat;
Weak as a lamb the hour that it is yeaned;
And white with foam as if with cleaving sleet.

Upon his side the hart was lying stretched:
His nostril touched a spring beneath a hill,
And with the last deep groan his breath had fetched
The waters of the spring were trembling still.   20

And now, too happy for repose or rest,
(Never had living man such joyful lot!)
Sir Walter walked all round, north, south, and west
And gazed and gazed upon that darling spot.

And climbing up the hill—(it was at least
Four roods of sheer ascent) Sir Walter found
Three several hoof-marks which the hunted beast
Had left imprinted on the grassy ground.

Sir Walter wiped his face, and cried, " Till now
Such sight was never seen by human eyes: 30
Three leaps have borne him from this lofty brow
Down to the very fountain where he lies.

HART-LEAP WELL

" I'll build a pleasure-house upon this spot,
And a small arbour, made for rural joy ;
'Twill be the traveller's shed, the pilgrim's cot,
A place of love for damsels that are coy.

" A cunning artist will I have to frame
A basin for that fountain in the dell !
And they who do make mention of the same,
From this day forth, shall call it HART-LEAP WELL.

" And, gallant stag ! to make thy praises known,
Another monument shall here be raised ;   10
Three several pillars, each a rough-hewn stone,
And planted where thy hoofs the turf have grazed.

" And in the summer-time, when days are long,
I will come hither with my paramour ;
And with the dancers and the minstrel's song
We will make merry in that pleasant bower.

" Till the foundations of the mountains fail
My mansion with its arbour shall endure ;—
The joy of them who till the fields of Swale,
And them who dwell among the woods of Ure ! " 20

Then home he went, and left the hart stone-dead,
With breathless nostrils stretched above the spring.
—Soon did the Knight perform what he had said ;
And far and wide the fame thereof did ring.

Ere thrice the moon into her port had steered,
A cup of stone received the living well ;
Three pillars of rude stone Sir Walter reared,
And built a house of pleasure in the dell.

And, near the fountain, flowers of stature tall
With trailing plants and trees were intertwined,— 30
Which soon composed a little sylvan hall,
A leafy shelter from the sun and wind.

POEMS OLD AND NEW

And thither, when the summer days were long,
Sir Walter led his wondering paramour ;
And with the dancers and the minstrel's song
Made merriment within that pleasant bower.

The Knight, Sir Walter, died in course of time,
And his bones lie in his paternal vale.—
But there is matter for a second rhyme,
And I to this would add another tale.

Part Second

The moving accident is not my trade ;
To freeze the blood I have no ready arts :　　　10
'Tis my delight, along in summer shade,
To pipe a simple song for thinking hearts.

As I from Hawes to Richmond did repair,
It chanced that I saw standing in a dell
Three aspens at three corners of a square ;
And one, not four yards distant, near a well.

What this imported I could ill divine :
And, pulling now the rein my horse to stop,
I saw three pillars standing in a line,—
The last stone-pillar on a dark hill-top.　　　20

The trees were grey, with neither arms nor head ;
Half wasted the square mound of tawny green ;
So that you just might say, as then I said,
" Here in old time the hand of man hath been."

I looked upon the hill both far and near,
More doleful place did never eye survey ;
It seemed as if the spring-time came not here,
And Nature here were willing to decay.

HART-LEAP WELL

I stood in various thoughts and fancies lost,
When one, who was in shepherd's garb attired,
Came up the hollow :—him did I accost,
And what this place might be I then inquired.

The Shepherd stopped, and that same story told
Which in my former rhyme I have rehearsed.
" A jolly place," said he, " in times of old !
But something ails it now : the spot is curst.

" You see these lifeless stumps of aspen wood—
Some say that they are beeches, other elms— 10
These were the bower ; and here a mansion stood,
The finest palace of a hundred realms !

" The arbour does its own condition tell ;
You see the stones, the fountain, and the stream ;
But as to the great Lodge ! you might as well
Hunt half a day for a forgotten dream.

" There's neither dog nor heifer, horse nor sheep,
Will wet his lips within that cup of stone ;
And oftentimes, when all are fast asleep,
This water doth send forth a dolorous groan. 20

" Some say that here a murder has been done,
And blood cries out for blood : but, for my part,
I've guessed, when I've been sitting in the sun,
That it was all for that unhappy hart.

" What thoughts must through the creature's brain
      have past !
Even from the topmost stone, upon the steep,
Are but three bounds—and look, Sir, at this last—
O Master ! it has been a cruel leap.

POEMS OLD AND NEW

" For thirteen hours he ran a desperate race ;
And in my simple mind we cannot tell
What cause the hart might have to love this place,
And come and make his death-bed near the well.

" Here on the grass perhaps asleep he sank,
Lulled by the fountain in the summer-tide ;
This water was perhaps the first he drank
When he had wandered from his mother's side.

" In April here, beneath the flowering thorn,
He heard the birds their morning carols sing ; 10
And he perhaps, for aught we know, was born
Not half a furlong from that self-same spring.

" Now, here is neither grass nor pleasant shade;
The sun on drearier hollow never shone ;
So will it be, as I have often said,
Till trees, and stones, and fountain, all are gone."

" Grey-headed shepherd, thou hast spoken well ;
Small difference lies between thy creed and mine :
This beast not unobserved by Nature fell ;
His death was mourned by sympathy divine. 20

" The Being that is in the clouds and air,
That is in the green leaves among the groves,
Maintains a deep and reverential care
For the unoffending creatures whom he loves.

' The pleasure-house is dust :—behind, before,
This is no common waste, no common gloom ;
But Nature, in due course of time, once more
Shall here put on her beauty and her bloom.

' She leaves these objects to a slow decay,
That what we are, and have been, may be known ; 30
But at the coming of the milder day
These monuments shall all be overgrown.

THE DESTRUCTION OF SENNACHERIB

" One lesson, shepherd, let us two divide,
Taught both by what she shows, and what conceals ;
Never to blend our pleasure or our pride
With sorrow of the meanest thing that feels."
     WILLIAM WORDSWORTH

THE DESTRUCTION OF SENNACHERIB

THE Assyrian came down like the wolf on the fold,
And his cohorts were gleaming in purple and gold ;
And the sheen of their spears was like stars on the sea,
When the blue wave rolls nightly on deep Galilee.

Like the leaves of the forest when Summer is green,
That host with their banners at sunset were seen : 10
Like the leaves of the forest when Autumn hath blown,
That host on the morrow lay wither'd and strown.

For the Angel of Death spread his wings on the blast,
And breathed in the face of the foe as he pass'd ;
And the eyes of the sleepers wax'd deadly and chill,
And their hearts but once heaved, and for ever grew still !

And there lay the steed with his nostril all wide,
But through it there roll'd not the breath of his pride ;
And the foam of his gasping lay white on the turf,
And cold as the spray of the rock-beating surf.   20

And there lay the rider distorted and pale,
With the dew on his brow, and the rust on his mail :
And the tents were all silent, the banners alone,
The lances unlifted, the trumpet unblown.

POEMS OLD AND NEW

And the widows of Ashur are loud in their wail,
And the idols are broke in the temple of Baal ;
And the might of the Gentile, unsmote by the sword,
Hath melted like snow in the glance of the Lord !
LORD BYRON

THE ARMADA

ATTEND, all ye who list to hear our noble England's praise ; 5
I tell of the thrice-famous deeds she wrought in ancient days,
When that great fleet invincible against her bore in vain
The richest spoils of Mexico, the stoutest hearts of Spain.

It was about the lovely close of a warm summer day,
There came a gallant merchant-ship full sail to Plymouth Bay ; 10
Her crew had seen Castile's black fleet, beyond Aurigny's Isle,
At earliest twilight, on the waves lie heaving many a mile.
At sunrise she escaped their van, by God's especial grace ;
And the tall Pinta, till the noon, had held her close in chase.
Forthwith a guard at every gun was placed along the wall ; 15
The beacon blazed upon the roof of Edgecumbe's lofty hall ;
Many a light fishing bark put out to pry along the coast,
And with loose rein and bloody spur rode inland many a post.

THE ARMADA

With his white hair unbonneted, the stout old sheriff comes;
Behind him march the halberdiers; before him sound the drums;
His yeomen round the market cross make clear an ample space;
For there behoves him to set up the standard of Her Grace.
And haughtily the trumpets peal, and gaily dance the bells,   5
As slow upon the labouring wind the royal blazon swells.
Look how the Lion of the sea lifts up his ancient crown,
And underneath his deadly paw treads the gay lilies down.
So stalked he when he turned to flight, on that famed Picard field,
Bohemia's plume, and Genoa's bow, and Caesar's eagle shield.   10
So glared he when at Agincourt in wrath he turned to bay,
And crushed and torn beneath his claws the princely hunters lay.
Ho! strike the flagstaff deep, Sir Knight: ho! scatter flowers, fair maids:
Ho! gunners, fire a loud salute: ho! gallants, draw your blades:
Thou sun, shine on her joyously; ye breezes, waft her wide;   15
Our glorious SEMPER EADEM, the banner of our pride.
The freshening breeze of eve unfurled that banner's massy fold;
The parting gleam of sunshine kissed that haughty scroll of gold;
Night sank upon the dusky beach, and on the purple sea,

POEMS OLD AND NEW

Such night in England ne'er had been, nor e'er again shall be.
From Eddystone to Berwick bounds, from Lynn to Milford Bay,
That time of slumber was as bright and busy as the day;
For swift to east and swift to west the ghastly war-flame spread,
High on St. Michael's Mount it shone : it shone on Beachy Head. 5
Far on the deep the Spaniard saw, along each southern shire,
Cape beyond cape, in endless range, those twinkling points of fire.
The fisher left his skiff to rock on Tamar's glittering waves :
The rugged miners poured to war from Mendip's sunless caves :
O'er Longleat's towers, o'er Cranbourne's oaks, the fiery herald flew : 10
He roused the shepherds of Stonehenge, the rangers of Beaulieu.
Right sharp and quick the bells all night rang out from Bristol town,
And ere the day three hundred horse had met on Clifton Down ;
The sentinel on Whitehall gate looked forth into the night,
And saw o'erhanging Richmond Hill the streak of blood-red light ; 15
Then bugle's note and cannon's roar the death-like silence broke,
And with one start, and with one cry, the royal city woke.
At once on all her stately gates arose the answering fires ;
At once the wild alarum clashed from all her reeling spires ;

THE ARMADA

From all the batteries of the Tower pealed loud
  the voice of fear ;
And all the thousand masts of Thames sent back
  a louder cheer ;
And from the furthest wards was heard the rush
  of hurrying feet,
And the broad streams of pikes and flags rushed
  down each roaring street ;
And broader still became the blaze, and louder still
  the din,   5
As fast from every village round the horse came
  spurring in :
And eastward straight from wild Blackheath the
  warlike errand went,
And roused in many an· ancient hall the gallant
  squires of Kent.
Southward from Surrey's pleasant hills flew those
  bright couriers forth ;
High on bleak Hampstead's swarthy moor they
  started for the north ;   10
And on, and on, without a pause, untired they
  bounded still :
All night from tower to tower they sprang ; they
  sprang from hill to hill :
Till the proud Peak unfurled the flag o'er Darwin's
  rocky dales,
Till like volcanoes flared to heaven the stormy hills
  of Wales,
Till twelve fair counties saw the blaze on Malvern's
  lonely height,   15
Till streamed in crimson on the wind the Wrekin's
  crest of light,
Till broad and fierce the star came forth on Ely's
  stately fane,
And tower and hamlet rose in arms o'er all the
  boundless plain ;
Till Belvoir's lordly terraces the sign to Lincoln sent,

POEMS OLD AND NEW

And Lincoln sped the message on o'er the wide vale
of Trent ;
Till Skiddaw saw the fire that burned on Gaunt's
embattled pile,
And the red glare on Skiddaw roused the burghers
of Carlisle.
LORD MACAULAY

MORTE D'ARTHUR

So all day long the noise of battle roll'd
Among the mountains by the winter sea ;
Until King Arthur's table, man by man,
Had fall'n in Lyonnesse about their lord,
King Arthur : then, because his wound was deep,
The bold Sir Bedivere uplifted him,
Sir Bedivere, the last of all his knights,   10
And bore him to a chapel nigh the field,
A broken chancel with a broken cross,
That stood on a dark strait of barren land.
On one side lay the Ocean, and on one
Lay a great water, and the moon was full.
   Then spake King Arthur to Sir Bedivere :
" The sequel of to-day unsolders all
The goodliest fellowship of famous knights
Whereof this world holds record. Such a sleep
They sleep—the men I loved. I think that we   20
Shall never more, at any future time,
Delight our souls with talk of knightly deeds,
Walking about the gardens and the halls
Of Camelot, as in the days that were.
I perish by this people which I made,—
Tho' Merlin sware that I should come again
To rule once more—but let what will be, be,
I am so deeply smitten thro' the helm
That without help I cannot last till morn.

MORTE D'ARTHUR

Thou therefore take my brand Excalibur,
Which was my pride : for thou rememberest how
In those old days, one summer noon, an arm
Rose up from out the bosom of the lake,
Clothed in white samite, mystic, wonderful,
Holding the sword—and how I row'd across
And took it, and have worn it, like a king :
And, wheresoever I am sung or told
In aftertime, this also shall be known :
But now delay not : take Excalibur,   10
And fling him far into the middle mere :
Watch what thou seëst, and lightly bring me word."
   To him replied the bold Sir Bedivere :
" It is not meet, Sir King, to leave thee thus,
Aidless, alone, and smitten thro' the helm.
A little thing may harm a wounded man.
Yet I thy hest will all perform at full,
Watch what I see, and lightly bring thee word."
   So saying, from the ruin'd shrine he stept,
And in the moon athwart the place of tombs,   20
Where lay the mighty bones of ancient men.
Old knights, and over them the sea-wind sang
Shrill, chill, with flakes of foam. He, stepping down
By zigzag paths, and juts of pointed rock,
Came on the shining levels of the lake.
   There drew he forth the brand Excalibur,
And o'er him, drawing it, the winter moon,
Brightening the skirts of a long cloud, ran forth
And sparkled keen with frost against the hilt :
For all the haft twinkled with diamond sparks,   30
Myriads of topaz-lights, and jacinth-work
Of subtlest jewellery. He gazed so long
That both his eyes were dazzled, as he stood,
This way and that dividing the swift mind,
In act to throw : but at the last it seem'd
Better to leave Excalibur conceal'd
There in the many-knotted waterflags,

That whistled stiff and dry about the marge.
So strode he back slow to the wounded king.
  Then spake King Arthur to Sir Bedivere :
" Hast thou perform'd my mission which I gave ?
What is it thou hast seen ? or what hast heard ? "
  And answer made the bold Sir Bedivere :
" I heard the ripple washing in the reeds,
And the wild water lapping on the crag."
  To whom replied King Arthur, faint and pale :
" Thou hast betray'd thy nature and thy name,   10
Not rendering true answer, as beseem'd
  Thy feälty, nor like a noble knight :
For surer sign had follow'd, either hand,
Or voice, or else a motion of the mere.
This is a shameful thing for men to lie.
Yet now, I charge thee, quickly go again
As thou art lief and dear, and do the thing
I bad thee, watch, and lightly bring me word."
  Then went Sir Bedivere the second time
Across the ridge, and paced beside the mere,   20
Counting the dewy pebbles, fix'd in thought ;
But when he saw the wonder of the hilt,
How curiously and strangely chased, he smote
His palms together, and he cried aloud :
  " And if indeed I cast the brand away,
Surely a precious thing, one worthy note,
Should thus be lost for ever from the earth,
Which might have pleased the eyes of many men.
What good should follow this, if this were done ?
What harm, undone ? deep harm to disobey,   30
Seeing obedience is the bond of rule.
Were it well to obey then, if a king demand
An act unprofitable, against himself ?
The King is sick, and knows not what he does.
What record, or what relic of my lord
Should be to aftertime, but empty breath
And rumours of a doubt ? but were this kept,

MORTE D'ARTHUR

Stored in some treasure-house of mighty kings,
Some one might show it at a joust of arms,
Saying, ' King Arthur's sword, Excalibur,
Wrought by the lonely maiden of the Lake.
Nine years she wrought it, sitting in the deeps
Upon the hidden bases of the hills.'
So might some old man speak in the aftertime
To all the people, winning reverence.
But now much honour and much fame were lost."
    So spake he, clouded with his own conceit,   10
And hid Excalibur the second time,
And so strode back slow to the wounded King.
    Then spoke King Arthur, breathing heavily :
" What is it thou hast seen ? or what hast heard ? "
    And answer made the bold Sir Bedivere :
" I heard the water lapping on the crag,
And the long ripple washing in the reeds."
    To whom replied King Arthur, much in wrath :
" Ah, miserable and unkind, untrue,
Unknightly, traitor-hearted ! Woe is me !   20
Authority forgets a dying king,
Laid widow'd of the power in his eye
That bow'd the will. I see thee what thou art,
For thou, the latest-left of all my knights,
In whom should meet the offices of all,
Thou wouldst betray me for the precious hilt ;
Either from lust of gold, or like a girl
Valuing the giddy pleasure of the eyes.
Yet, for a man may fail in duty twice,
And the third time may prosper, get thee hence :   30
But, if thou spare to fling Excalibur,
I will arise and slay thee with my hands."
    Then quickly rose Sir Bedivere, and ran,
And, leaping down the ridges lightly, plunged
Among the bulrush-beds, and clutch'd the sword,
And strongly wheel'd and threw it. The great brand
Made lightnings in the splendour of the moon,

And flashing round and round, and whirl'd in an arch,
Shot like a streamer of the northern morn,
Seen where the moving isles of winter shock
By night, with noises of the northern sea.
So flash'd and fell the brand Excalibur :
But ere he dipt the surface, rose an arm
Clothed in white samite, mystic, wonderful,
And caught him by the hilt, and brandish'd him
Three times, and drew him under in the mere.
And lightly went the other to the King. 10
    Then spoke King Arthur, drawing thicker breath :
" Now see I by thine eyes that this is done.
Speak out : what is it thou hast heard, or seen ? "
    And answer made the bold Sir Bedivere :
" Sir King, I closed mine eyelids, lest the gems
Should blind my purpose, for I never saw,
Nor shall see, here or elsewhere, till I die,
Not tho' I live three lives of mortal men,
So great a miracle as yonder hilt.
Then with both hands I flung him, wheeling him ; 20
But when I look'd again, behold an arm,
Clothed in white samite, mystic, wonderful,
That caught him by the hilt, and brandish'd him
Three times, and drew him under in the mere."
    And answer made King Arthur, breathing hard :
" My end draws nigh ; 'tis time that I were gone.
Make broad thy shoulders to receive my weight,
And bear me to the margin ; yet I fear
My wound hath taken cold, and I shall die."
    So saying, from the pavement he half rose, 30
Slowly, with pain, reclining on his arm,
And looking wistfully with wide blue eyes
As in a picture. Him Sir Bedivere
Remorsefully regarded thro' his tears,
And would have spoken, but he found not words,
Then took with care, and kneeling on one knee,
O'er both his shoulders drew the languid hands,

MORTE D'ARTHUR

And rising bore him thro' the place of tombs.
  But, as he walk'd, King Arthur panted hard,
Like one that feels a nightmare on his bed
When all the house is mute. So sigh'd the King,
Muttering and murmuring at his ear, " Quick, quick !
I fear it is too late, and I shall die."
But the other swiftly strode from ridge to ridge,
Clothed with his breath, and looking, as he walk'd,
Larger than human on the frozen hills.
He heard the deep behind him, and a cry   10
Before. His own thought drove him, like a goad.
Dry clash'd his harness in the icy caves
And barren chasms, and all to left and right
The bare black cliff clang'd round him, as he based
His feet on juts of slippery crag that rang
Sharp-smitten with the dint of armèd heels—
And on a sudden, lo ! the level lake,
And the long glories of the winter moon.
  Then saw they how there hove a dusky barge,
Dark as a funeral scarf from stem to stern,   20
Beneath them ; and descending they were ware
That all the decks were dense with stately forms,
Black-stoled, black-hooded, like a dream—by these
Three Queens with crowns of gold—and from them rose
A cry that shiver'd to the tingling stars,
And, as it were one voice, an agony
Of lamentation, like a wind, that shrills
All night in a waste land, where no one comes,
Or hath come, since the making of the world.
  Then murmur'd Arthur, " Place me in the barge," 30
And to the barge they came. There those three Queens
Put forth their hands, and took the King, and wept.
But she, that rose the tallest of them all
And fairest, laid his head upon her lap,
And loosed the shatter'd casque, and chafed his hands,

45

And call'd him by his name, complaining loud,
And dropping bitter tears against his brow
Striped with dark blood : for all his face was white
And colourless, and like the wither'd moon
Smote by the fresh beam of the springing east ;
And all his greaves and cuisses dash'd with drops
Of onset ; and the light and lustrous curls—
That made his forehead like a rising sun
High from the daïs-throne—were parch'd with dust ;
Or, clotted into points and hanging loose,   10
Mix'd with the knightly growth that fringed his lips.
So like a shatter'd column lay the King ;
Not like that Arthur who, with lance in rest,
From spur to plume a star of tournament,
Shot thro' the lists at Camelot, and charged
Before the eyes of ladies and of kings.
  Then loudly cried the bold Sir Bedivere :
" Ah ! my Lord Arthur, whither shall I go ?
Where shall I hide my forehead and my eyes ?
For now I see the true old times are dead,   20
When every morning brought a noble chance,
And every chance brought out a noble knight.
Such times have been not since the light that led
The holy Elders with the gift of myrrh.
But now the whole ROUND TABLE is dissolved
Which was an image of the mighty world ;
And I, the last, go forth companionless,
And the days darken round me, and the years,
Among new men, strange faces, other minds."
  And slowly answer'd Arthur from the barge :   30
" The old order changeth, yielding place to new,
And God fulfils Himself in many ways,
Lest one good custom should corrupt the world.
Comfort thyself : what comfort is in me ?
I have lived my life, and that which I have done
May He within Himself make pure ! but thou,
If thou shouldst never see my face again,

THE LADY OF SHALOTT

'ray for my soul. More things are wrought by prayer
Than this world dreams of. Wherefore, let thy voice
Rise like a fountain for me night and day.
For what are men better than sheep or goats
That nourish a blind life within the brain,
If, knowing God, they lift not hands of prayer
Both for themselves and those who call them friend ?
For so the whole round earth is every way
Bound by gold chains about the feet of God.
But now farewell. I am going a long way   10
With these thou seëst—if indeed I go—
(For all my mind is clouded with a doubt)
To the island-valley of Avilion ;
Where falls not hail, or rain, or any snow,
Nor ever wind blows loudly ; but it lies
Deep-meadow'd, happy, fair with orchard-lawns
And bowery hollows crown'd with summer sea,
Where I will heal me of my grievous wound."
    So said he, and the barge with oar and sail
Moved from the brink, like some full-breasted swan 20
That, fluting a wild carol ere her death,
Ruffles her pure cold plume, and takes the flood
With swarthy webs. Long stood Sir Bedivere
Revolving many memories, till the hull
Look'd one black dot against the verge of dawn,
And on the mere the wailing died away.
                                    LORD TENNYSON

THE LADY OF SHALOTT

PART I

On either side the river lie
Long fields of barley and of rye,
That clothe the wold and meet the sky ;
And thro' the field the road runs by   30
    To many-tower'd Camelot ;

And up and down the people go,
Gazing where the lilies blow
Round an island there below,
      The island of Shalott.

Willows whiten, aspens quiver,
Little breezes dusk and shiver
Thro' the wave that runs for ever
By the island in the river
      Flowing down to Camelot.
Four gray walls, and four gray towers,   10
Overlook a space of flowers,
And the silent isle imbowers
      The Lady of Shalott.

By the margin, willow-veil'd,
Slide the heavy barges trail'd
By slow horses ; and unhail'd
The shallop flitteth silken-sail'd
      Skimming down to Camelot :
But who hath seen her wave her hand ?
Or at the casement seen her stand ?   20
Or is she known in all the land,
      The Lady of Shalott ?

Only reapers, reaping early
In among the bearded barley,
Hear a song that echoes cheerly
From the river winding clearly,
      Down to tower'd Camelot :
And by the moon the reaper weary,
Piling sheaves in uplands airy,
Listening, whispers " 'Tis the fairy   30
      Lady of Shalott."

THE LADY OF SHALOTT

PART II

There she weaves by night and day
A magic web with colours gay.
She has heard a whisper say,
A curse is on her if she stay
      To look down to Camelot.
She knows not what the curse may be,
And so she weaveth steadily,
And little other care hath she,
      The Lady of Shalott.

And moving thro' a mirror clear   10
That hangs before her all the year,
Shadows of the world appear.
There she sees the highway near
      Winding down to Camelot :
There the river eddy whirls,
And there the surly village-churls,
And the red cloaks of market girls,
      Pass onward from Shalott.

Sometimes a troop of damsels glad,
An abbot on an ambling pad,   20
Sometimes a curly shepherd-lad,
Or long-hair'd page in crimson clad,
      Goes by to tower'd Camelot ;
And sometimes thro' the mirror blue
The knights come riding two and two :
She hath no loyal knight and true,
      The Lady of Shalott.

But in her web she still delights
To weave the mirror's magic sights,
For often thro' the silent nights   30
A funeral, with plumes and lights
      And music, went to Camelot :

Or when the moon was overhead,
Came two young lovers lately wed ;
" I am half sick of shadows," said
    The Lady of Shalott.

Part III

A bow-shot from her bower-eaves,
He rode between the barley-sheaves,
The sun came dazzling thro' the leaves,
And flamed upon the brazen greaves
    Of bold Sir Lancelot.
A red-cross knight for ever kneel'd
To a lady in his shield,
That sparkled on the yellow field
    Beside remote Shalott.

The gemmy bridle glitter'd free,
Like to some branch of stars we see
Hung in the golden Galaxy.
The bridle bells rang merrily
    As he rode down to Camelot :
And from his blazon'd baldric slung
A mighty silver bugle hung,
And as he rode his armour rung,
    Beside remote Shalott.

All in the blue unclouded weather
Thick-jewell'd shone the saddle-leather,
The helmet and the helmet-feather
Burn'd like one burning flame together,
    As he rode down to Camelot.
As often thro' the purple night,
Below the starry clusters bright,
Some bearded meteor, trailing light,
    Moves over still Shalott.

THE LADY OF SHALOTT

His broad clear brow in sunlight glow'd ;
On burnish'd hooves his war-horse trode ;
From underneath his helmet flow'd
His coal-black curls as on he rode,
   As he rode down to Camelot.
From the bank and from the river
He flash'd into the crystal mirror,
" Tirra lirra," by the river
   Sang Sir Lancelot.

She left the web, she left the loom, 10
She made three paces thro' the room,
She saw the water-lily bloom,
She saw the helmet and the plume,
   She look'd down to Camelot.
Out flew the web and floated wide ;
The mirror crack'd from side to side ;
" The curse is come upon me," cried
   The Lady of Shalott.

Part IV

In the stormy east-wind straining,
The pale yellow woods were waning, 20
The broad stream in his banks complain
 ing,
Heavily the low sky raining
   Over tower'd Camelot ;
Down she came and found a boat
Beneath a willow left afloat,
And round about the prow she wrote
   The Lady of Shalott.

And down the river's dim expanse—
Like some bold seer in a trance,
Seeing all his own mischance— 30

With a glassy countenance
      Did she look to Camelot.
And at the closing of the day
She loosed the chain, and down she lay ;
The broad stream bore her far away,
      The Lady of Shalott.

Lying, robed in snowy white
That loosely flew to left and right—
The leaves upon her falling light—
Thro' the noises of the night   10
      She floated down to Camelot :
And as the boat-head wound along
The willowy hills and fields among,
They heard her singing her last song,
      The Lady of Shalott.

Heard a carol, mournful, holy,
Chanted loudly, chanted lowly,
Till her blood was frozen slowly,
And her eyes were darkened wholly,
      Turn'd to tower'd Camelot ;   20
For ere she reach'd upon the tide
The first house by the water-side,
Singing in her song she died,
      The Lady of Shalott.

Under tower and balcony,
By garden-wall and gallery,
A gleaming shape she floated by,
Dead-pale between the houses high,
      Silent into Camelot.
Out upon the wharfs they came,   30
Knight and burgher, lord and dame,
And round the prow they read her name,
      The Lady of Shalott.

HERVÉ RIEL

Who is this ? and what is here ?
And in the lighted palace near
Died the sound of royal cheer ;
And they cross'd themselves for fear,
    All the knights at Camelot :
But Lancelot mused a little space ;
  He said, " She has a lovely face ;
God in his mercy lend her grace,
    The Lady of Shalott."
              LORD TENNYSON

HERVÉ RIEL

ON the sea and at the Hogue, sixteen hundred ninety-
   two,
Did the English fight the French,—woe to France !
And, the thirty-first of May, helter-skelter thro' the
   blue,
Like a crowd of frightened porpoises a shoal of
   sharks pursue,
Came crowding ship on ship to St. Malo on the
   Rance,
With the English fleet in view.

'Twas the squadron that escaped, with the victor
   in full chase ;
  First and foremost of the drove, in his great ship,
     Damfreville ;
    Close on him fled, great and small,
    Twenty-two good ships in all ;
And they signalled to the place
" Help the winners of a race !
  Get us guidance, give us harbour, take us quick—
   or, quicker still,
  Here's the English can and will ! "

Then the pilots of the place put out brisk and leapt
   on board ;
"Why, what hope or chance have ships like these
   to pass ? " laughed they :
"Rocks to starboard, rocks to port, all the passage
   scarred and scored,
Shall the *Formidable* here with her twelve and eighty
   guns
Think to make the river-mouth by the single
   narrow way,
Trust to enter where 'tis ticklish for a craft of twenty
   tons,
   And with flow at full beside ?
   Now, 'tis slackest ebb of tide.
   Reach the mooring ? Rather say,
While rock stands or water runs,   10
Not a ship will leave the bay ! "

Then was called a council straight.
Brief and bitter the debate :
"Here's the English at our heels ; would you have
   them take in tow
All that's left us of the fleet, linked together stern and
   bow,
For a prize to Plymouth Sound ?
Better run the ships aground ! "
   (Ended Damfreville his speech).
Not a minute more to wait !
   "Let the Captains all and each   20
   Shove ashore, then blow up, burn the vessels on
      the beach !
France must undergo her fate.

Give the word ! " But no such word
Was ever spoke or heard ;
   For up stood, for out stepped, for in struck amid
      all these

HERVÉ RIEL

—A Captain ? A Lieutenant ? A Mate—first, second, third ?
No such man of mark, and meet
With his betters to compete !
But a simple Breton sailor pressed by Tourville for the fleet,
A poor coasting-pilot he, Hervé Riel the Croisickese.

And, " What mockery or malice have we here ? " cries Hervé Riel :
" Are you mad, you Malouins ? Are you cowards, fools, or rogues ?
Talk to me of rocks and shoals, me who took the soundings, tell
On my fingers every bank, every shallow, every swell
'Twixt the offing here and Grève where the river disembogues ?   10
Are you bought by English gold ? Is it love the lying's for ?
    Morn and eve, night and day,
    Have I piloted your bay,
Entered free and anchored fast at the foot of Solidor.

Burn the fleet and ruin France ? That were worse than fifty Hogues !
Sirs, they know I speak the truth ! Sirs, believe me there's a way !
Only let me lead the line,
    Have the biggest ship to steer,
    Get this *Formidable* clear,
Make the others follow mine,   20
And I lead them, most and least, by a passage I know well,
    Right to Solidor past Grève,

   · And there lay them safe and sound ;
   And if one ship misbehave,
    —Keel so much as grate the ground,
Why, I've nothing but my life,—here's my head ! "
   cries Hervé Riel.

   Not a minute more to wait.
" Steer us in, then, small and great !
   Take the helm, lead the line, save the squadron ! "
   cried its chief.
" Captains, give the sailor place !
   He is Admiral, in brief."
Still the north-wind, by God's grace !
See the noble fellow's face,
As the big ship with a bound,
Clears the entry like a hound,
Keeps the passage as its inch of way were the wide
   seas profound !
   See, safe thro' shoal and rock,
   How they follow in a flock,
Not a ship that misbehaves, not a keel that grates the
   ground,
   Not a spar that comes to grief !
The peril, see, is past,
All are harboured to the last,
And just as Hervé Riel hollas " Anchor ! "—sure as
   fate
Up the English come, too late !

So, the storm subsides to calm :
   They see the green trees wave
   On the o'erlooking Grève.
Hearts that bled are stanched with balm.
" Just our rapture to enhance,
   Let the English rake the bay,
Gnash their teeth and glare askance,
   As they cannonade away !

HERVÉ RIEL

'Neath rampired Solidor pleasant riding on the
    Rance ! "
How hope succeeds despair on each Captain's coun-
    tenance !
Out burst all with one accord,
" This is Paradise for Hell !
    Let France, let France's King
    Thank the man that did the thing ! "
What a shout, and all one word,
" Hervé Riel ! "
As he stepped in front once more,
    Not a symptom of surprise   10
    In the frank blue Breton eyes,
Just the same man as before.

Then said Damfreville, " My friend,
I must speak out at the end,
    Though I find the speaking hard.
Praise is deeper than the lips :
You have saved the King his ships,
    You must name your own reward.
'Faith our sun was near eclipse !
Demand whate'er you will,   20
France remains your debtor still.
Ask to heart's content and have ! or my name's not
    Damfreville."

Then a beam of fun outbroke
On the bearded mouth that spoke,
As the honest heart laughed through
Those frank eyes of Breton blue :
" Since I needs must say my say,
    Since on board the duty's done,
        And from Malo Roads to Croisic Point, what is it
            but a run ?—
Since 'tis ask and have, I may—   30
    Since the others go ashore—

Come ! A good whole holiday !
Leave to go and see my wife, whom I call the
    Belle Aurore ! "
That he asked and that he got,—nothing more.

Name and deed alike are lost :
Not a pillar nor a post
    In his Croisic keeps alive the feat as it befell ;
Not a head in white and black
On a single fishing smack,
    In memory of the man but for whom had gone to
        wrack
    All that France saved from the fight whence
        England bore the bell.
Go to Paris : rank on rank
    Search the heroes flung pell-mell
On the Louvre, face and flank !
    You shall look long enough ere you come to
        Hervé Riel.
So, for better and for worse,
Hervé Riel, accept my verse !
In my verse, Hervé Riel, do thou once more
Save the squadron, honour France, love thy wife, the
    Belle Aurore !
                                    ROBERT BROWNING

THE PIED PIPER OF HAMELIN

A Child's Story

Hamelin Town's in Brunswick,
    By famous Hanover city ;
The river Weser, deep and wide,
Washes its wall on the southern side ;
A pleasanter spot you never spied ;

THE PIED PIPER OF HAMELIN

But, when begins my ditty,
Almost five hundred years ago,
To see the townsfolk suffer so
From vermin, was a pity.

Rats !
They fought the dogs, and killed the cats,
  And bit the babies in the cradles,
And ate the cheeses out of the vats,
  And licked the soup from the cooks' own ladles,
Split open the kegs of salted sprats,   10
Made nests inside men's Sunday hats,
And even spoiled the women's chats
    By drowning their speaking
    With shrieking and squeaking
In fifty different sharps and flats.

At last the people in a body
  To the Town Hall came flocking :
" 'Tis clear," cried they, " our mayor's a noddy ;
  And as for our Corporation—shocking
To think we buy gowns lined with ermine   20
For dolts that can't or won't determine
What's best to rid us of our vermin !
You hope, because you're old and obese,
To find in the furry civic robe ease ?
Rouse up, Sirs ! Give your brains a racking
To find the remedy we're lacking,
Or, sure as fate, we'll send you packing ! "
At this the Mayor and Corporation
Quaked with a mighty consternation.

An hour they sate in council ;   30
  At length the Mayor broke silence :
" For a guilder I'd my ermine gown sell,
  I wish I were a mile hence !
It's easy to bid one rack one's brain—

I'm sure my poor head aches again
I've scratched it so, and all in vain.
Oh for a trap, a trap, a trap ! "
Just as he said this, what should hap
At the chamber door but a gentle tap ?
" Bless us," cried the Mayor, " what's that ? "
(With the Corporation as he sat,
Looking little though wondrous fat ;
Nor brighter was his eye, nor moister
Than a too-long-opened oyster,   10
Save when at noon his paunch grew mutinous
For a plate of turtle green and glutinous)
" Only a scraping of shoes on the mat ?
Anything like the sound of a rat
Makes my heart go pit-a-pat ! "

" Come in ! "—the Mayor cried, looking bigger :
And in did come the strangest figure !
His queer long coat from heel to head
Was half of yellow and half of red ;
And he himself was tall and thin,   20
With sharp blue eyes, each like a pin,
And light loose hair, yet swarthy skin,
No tuft on cheek nor beard on chin,
But lips where smiles went out and in—
There was no guessing-his kith and kin !
And nobody could enough admire
The tall man and his quaint attire.
Quoth one : " It's as my great grandsire,
Starting up at the Trump of Doom's tone,
Had walked this way from his painted tomb-stone ! "

He advanced to the council-table :   31
And, " Please your honours," said he, " I'm able,
By means of a secret charm, to draw
All creatures living beneath the sun,
That creep or swim or fly or run,

THE PIED PIPER OF HAMELIN

After me so as you never saw !
And I chiefly use my charm
On creatures that do people harm,
The mole and toad and newt and viper ;
And people call me the Pied Piper."
(And here they noticed round his neck
   A scarf of red and yellow stripe,
To match with his coat of the self-same cheque ;
   And at the scarf's end hung a pipe ;
And his fingers, they noticed, were ever straying 10
As if impatient to be playing
Upon this pipe as low it dangled
Over his vesture so old-fangled.)
" Yet," said he, " poor piper as I am,
In Tartary I freed the Cham,
   Last June, from his huge swarms of gnats :
I eased in Asia the Nizam
   Of a monstrous brood of vampyre-bats :
And as for what your brain bewilders,
   If I can rid your town of rats   20
Will you give me a thousand guilders ? "
" One ? fifty thousand ! "—was the exclamation
Of the astonished Mayor and Corporation.

Into the street the piper stept,
   Smiling first a little smile,
As if he knew what magic slept
   In his quiet pipe the while ;
Then, like a musical adept,
To blow the pipe his lips he wrinkled,
And green and blue his sharp eyes twinkled   30
Like a candle-flame where salt is sprinkled ;
And ere three shrill notes the pipe uttered,
You heard as if an army muttered ;
And the muttering grew to a grumbling ;
And the grumbling grew to a mighty rumbling ;

And out of the houses the rats came tumbling.
Great rats, small rats, lean rats, brawny rats,
Brown rats, black rats, grey rats, tawny rats,
Grave old plodders, gay young friskers,
　　Fathers, mothers, uncles, cousins,
Cocking tails and pricking whiskers,
　　Families by tens and dozens,
Brothers, sisters, husbands, wives—
Followed the Piper for their lives.
From street to street he piped advancing,
And step for step they followed dancing,
Until they came to the river Weser,
　　Wherein all plunged and perished !
—Save one who, stout as Julius Caesar,
Swam across and lived to carry
　　(As he, the manuscript he cherished)
To Rat-land home his commentary :
Which was, " At the first shrill notes of the
　　　　pipe,
I heard a sound as of scraping tripe,
And putting apples, wondrous ripe,
Into a cider-press's gripe :
And a moving away of pickle-tub-boards,
And a leaving ajar of conserve-cup-boards,
And a drawing the corks of train-oil flasks,
And a breaking the hoops of butter-casks :
And it seemed as if a voice
　　(Sweeter far than by harp or by psaltery
Is breathed) called out, ' Oh rats, rejoice !
　　The world is grown to one vast drysaltèry !
So munch on, crunch on, take your nuncheon,
Breakfast, supper, dinner, luncheon ! '
And just as a bulky sugar-puncheon,
All ready staved, like a great sun shone
Glorious scarce an inch before me,
Just as methought it said, ' Come, bore me ! '
—I found the Weser rolling o'er me."

THE PIED PIPER OF HAMELIN

You should have heard the Hamelin people
Ring the bells till they rocked the steeple.
" Go," cried the Mayor, " and get long poles !
Poke out the nests and block up the holes !
   Consult with carpenters and builders,
And leave in our town not even a trace
Of the rats ! "—when suddenly, up the face
Of the Piper perked in the market-place,
   With a, "First, if you please, my thousand guilders!"

A thousand guilders ! The Mayor looked blue ;   10
So did the Corporation too.
For council dinners made rare havoc
With Claret, Moselle, Vin-de-Grave, Hock ;
And half the money would replenish
Their cellar's biggest butt with Rhenish.
To pay this sum to a wandering fellow
With a gipsy coat of red and yellow !
" Besides," quoth the Mayor, with a knowing wink,
" Our business was done at the river's brink ;
We saw with our eyes the vermin sink,   20
And what's dead can't come to life, I think.
So, friend, we're not the folks to shrink
From the duty of giving you something for drink,
And a matter of money to put in your poke ;
But as for the guilders, what we spoke
Of them, as you very well know, was in joke.
Besides, our losses have made us thrifty !
A thousand guilders ! Come, take fifty ! "

The piper's face fell, and he cried,
" No trifling ! I can't wait, beside !   30
I've promised to visit by dinner time
Bagdat, and accept the prime
Of the Head-Cook's pottage, all he's rich in,
For having left, in the Caliph's kitchen,
Of a nest of scorpions no survivor :

63

POEMS OLD AND NEW

With him I proved no bargain-driver,
With you, don't think I'll bate a stiver !
And folks who put me in a passion
May find me pipe after another fashion."

" How ? " cried the Mayor, " d'ye think I'll brook
Being worse treated than a Cook ?
Insulted by a lazy ribald
With idle pipe and vesture piebald ?
You threaten us, fellow ? Do your worst,
Blow your pipe there till you burst ! "   10

Once more he stept into the street;
   And to his lips again
     Laid his long pipe of smooth straight cane ;
And ere he blew three notes (such sweet
Soft notes as yet musician's cunning
   Never gave the enraptured air)
There was a rustling that seemed like a bustling
Of merry crowds justling at pitching and hustling,
Small feet were pattering, wooden shoes clattering,
Little hands clapping and little tongues chattering,   20
And, like fowl in a farm-yard when barley is scattering,
Out came the children running.
All the little boys and girls,
With rosy cheeks and flaxen curls,
And sparkling eyes and teeth like pearls,
Tripping and skipping, ran merrily after
The wonderful music with shouting and laughter.

The Mayor was dumb, and the Council stood
As if they were changed into blocks of wood,
Unable to move a step, or cry   30
To the children merrily skipping by—
And could only follow with the eye
That joyous crowd at the Piper's back.
But how the Mayor was on the rack,

THE PIED PIPER OF HAMELIN

And the wretched Council's bosoms beat,
As the Piper turned from the High Street
To where the Weser rolled its waters
Right in the way of their sons and daughters !
However he turned from South to West,
And to Koppelberg Hill his steps addressed,
And after him the children pressed ;
Great was the joy in every breast.
" He never can cross that mighty top !
He's forced to let the piping drop,   10
And we shall see our children stop ! "
When, lo, as they reached the mountain's side,
A wondrous portal opened wide,
As if a cavern was suddenly hollowed ;
And the Piper advanced and the children followed,
And when all were in to the very last,
The door in the mountain-side shut fast.
Did I say, all ? No ! One was lame,
   And could not dance the whole of the way ;
And in after years, if you would blame   20
   His sadness, he was used to say,—
" It's dull in our town since my playmates left !
I can't forget that I'm bereft
Of all the pleasant sights they see,
Which the Piper also promised me.
For he led us, he said, to a joyous land,
Joining the town and just at hand,
Where waters gushed and fruit-trees grew,
And flowers put forth a fairer hue,
And everything was strange and new ;   30
The sparrows were brighter than peacocks here,
And their dogs outran our fallow deer,
And honey-bees had lost their stings,
And horses were born with eagles' wings :
And just as I became assured
My lame foot would be speedily cured,
The music stopped and I stood still,

And found myself outside the Hill,
Left alone against my will,
To go now limping as before,
And never hear of that country more ! "

Alas, alas for Hamelin !
  There came into many a burgher's pate
  A text which says that Heaven's Gate
  Opes to the Rich at as easy rate
As the needle's eye takes a camel in !
The Mayor sent East, West, North, and South,   10
To offer the Piper, by word of mouth,
  Wherever it was men's lot to find him,
Silver and gold to his heart's content,
If he'd only return the way he went,
  And bring the children behind him.
But when they saw 'twas a lost endeavour,
And Piper and dancers were gone for ever,
They made a decree that lawyers never
  Should think their records dated duly
If, after the day of the month and year,   20
These words did not as well appear,
" And so long after what happened here
  On the Twenty-second of July,
Thirteen hundred and seventy-six " :
And the better in memory to fix
The place of the children's last retreat,
They called it, the Pied Piper's Street—
Where any one playing on pipe or tabor
Was sure for the future to lose his labour.
Nor suffered they hostelry or tavern   30
  To shock with mirth a street so solemn ;
But opposite the place of the cavern
  They wrote the story on a column,
And on the great Church-Window painted
The same to make the world acquainted
How their children were stolen away ;

GOBLIN MARKET

And there it stands to this very day.
And I must not omit to say
That in Transylvania there's a tribe
Of alien people that ascribe
The outlandish ways and dress
On which their neighbours lay such stress,
To their fathers and mothers having risen
Out of some subterraneous prison
Into which they were trepanned
Long time ago in a mighty band   10
Out of Hamelin town in Brunswick land,
But how or why, they don't understand.

So, Willy, let you and me be wipers
Of scores out with all men—especially pipers:
And, whether they pipe us free from rats or fróm mice,
If we've promised them aught, let us keep our promise!
                                    ROBERT BROWNING

GOBLIN MARKET

Morning and evening
Maids heard the goblins cry:
" Come buy our orchard fruits,
Come buy, come buy: 5
Apples and quinces,
Lemons and oranges,
Plump unpecked cherries,
Melons and raspberries,
Bloom-down-cheeked peaches,
Swart-headed mulberries,
Wild free-born cranberries,
Crab-apples, dewberries,
Pine-apples, blackberries,
Apricots, strawberries;—

POEMS OLD AND NEW

All ripe together
In summer weather,—
Morns that pass by,
Fair eyes that fly ;
Come buy, come buy :
Our grapes fresh from the vine,
Pomegranates full and fine,
Dates and sharp bullaces,
Rare pears and greengages,
Damsons and bilberries,　　　　　　　　10
Taste them and try :
Currants and gooseberries,
Bright-fire-like barberries,
Figs to fill your mouth,
Citrons from the South,
Sweet to tongue and sound to eye ;
Come buy, come buy."

　　Evening by evening
Among the brookside rushes,
Laura bowed her head to hear,　　　　　20
Lizzie veiled her blushes :
Crouching close together
In the cooling weather,
With clasping arms and cautioning lips,
With tingling cheeks and finger tips.
" Lie close," Laura said,
Pricking up her golden head :
" We must not look at goblin men,
We must not buy their fruits :
Who knows upon what soil they fed　　　30
Their hungry thirsty roots ? "
" Come buy," call the goblins
Hobbling down the glen.
" Oh," cried Lizzie, " Laura, Laura,
You should not peep at goblin men."
Lizzie covered up her eyes,

68

GOBLIN MARKET

Covered close lest they should look ;
Laura reared her glossy head,
And whispered like the restless brook :
" Look, Lizzie, look, Lizzie,
Down the glen tramp little men.
One hauls a basket,
One bears a plate,
One lugs a golden dish
Of many pounds weight.
How fair the vine must grow   10
Whose grapes are so luscious ;
How warm the wind must blow
Through those fruit bushes."
" No," said Lizzie : " No, no, no ;
Their offers should not charm us,
Their evil gifts would harm us."
She thrust a dimpled finger
In each ear, shut eyes and ran :
Curious Laura chose to linger
Wondering at each merchant man.   20
One had a cat's face,
One whisked a tail,
One tramped at a rat's pace,
One crawled like a snail,
One like a wombat prowled obtuse and furry,
One like a ratel tumbled hurry skurry.
She heard a voice like voice of doves
Cooing all together :
They sounded kind and full of loves
In the pleasant weather.   30

    Laura stretched her gleaming neck
Like a rush-imbedded swan,
Like a lily from the beck,
Like a moonlit poplar branch,
Like a vessel at the launch
When its last restraint is gone.

Backwards up the mossy glen
Turned and trooped the goblin men
With their shrill repeated cry,
" Come buy, come buy."
When they reached where Laura was
They stood stock still upon the moss,
Leering at each other,
Brother with queer brother ;
Signalling each other,
Brother with sly brother.
One set his basket down,
One reared his plate ;
One began to weave a crown
Of tendrils, leaves, and rough nuts brown
(Men sell not such in any town) ;
One heaved the golden weight
Of dish and fruit to offer her :
" Come buy, come buy," was still their cry.
Laura stared but did not stir,
Longed but had no money :
The whisk-tailed merchant bade her taste
In tones as smooth as honey,
The cat-faced purr'd,
The rat-paced spoke a word
Of welcome, and the snail-paced even was heard ;
One parrot-voiced and jolly
Cried " Pretty Goblin " still for " Pretty Polly " ;—
One whistled like a bird.

But sweet-tooth Laura spoke in haste :
" Good folk, I have no coin ;
To take were to purloin :
I have no copper in my purse,
I have no silver either,
And all my gold is on the furze
That shakes in windy weather
Above the rusty heather."

GOBLIN MARKET

" You have much gold upon your head."
They answered all together :
" Buy from us with a golden curl."
She clipped a precious golden lock,
She dropped a tear more rare than pearl,
Then sucked their fruit globes fair or red :
Sweeter than honey from the rock,
Stronger than man-rejoicing wine,
Clearer than water flowed that juice ;
She never tasted such before,   10
How should it cloy with length of use ?
She sucked and sucked and sucked the more
Fruits which that unknown orchard bore ;
She sucked until her lips were sore ;
Then flung the emptied rinds away
But gathered up one kernel stone,
And knew not was it night or day
As she turned home alone.

   Lizzie met her at the gate
Full of wise upbraidings :   20
" Dear, you should not stay so late,
Twilight is not good for maidens ;
Should not loiter in the glen
In the haunts of goblin men.
Do you not remember Jeanie,
How she met them in the moonlight,
Took their gifts both choice and many,
Ate their fruits and wore their flowers
Plucked from bowers
Where summer ripens at all hours ?   30
But ever in the noonlight
She pined and pined away ;
Sought them by night and day,
Found them no more but dwindled and grew grey ;
Then fell with the first snow,
While to this day no grass will grow

Where she lies low :
I planted daisies there a year ago
That never blow.
You should not loiter so."
" Nay, hush," said Laura :
" Nay, hush, my sister :
I ate and ate my fill,
Yet my mouth waters still ;
To-morrow night I will
Buy more " : and kissed her : 10
" Have done with sorrow ;
I'll bring you plums to-morrow
Fresh on their mother twigs,
Cherries worth getting ;
You cannot think what figs
My teeth have met in,
What melons icy-cold
Piled on a dish of gold
Too huge for me to hold,
What peaches with a velvet nap, 20
Pellucid grapes without one seed :
Odorous indeed must be the mead
Whereon they grow, and pure the wave they drink
With lilies at the brink,
And sugar-sweet their sap."

    Golden head by golden head,
Like two pigeons in one nest,
Folded in each other's wings,
They lay down in their curtained bed :
Like two blossoms on one stem, 30
Like two flakes of new-fall'n snow,
Like two wands of ivory
Tipped with gold for awful kings.
Moon and stars gazed in at them,
Wind sang to them lullaby,
Lumbering owls forbore to fly,

GOBLIN MARKET

Not a bat flapped to and fro
Round their nest :
Cheek to cheek and breast to breast
Locked together in one nest.

Early in the morning
When the first cock crowed his warning,
Neat like bees, as sweet and busy,
Laura rose with Lizzie :
Fetched in honey, milked the cows,
Aired and set to rights the house,   10
Kneaded cakes of whitest wheat,
Cakes for dainty mouths to eat,
Next churned butter, whipped up cream,
Fed their poultry, sat and sewed ;
Talked as modest maidens should :
Lizzie with an open heart,
Laura in an absent dream,
One content, one sick in part ;
One warbling for the mere bright day's delight,
One longing for the night.   20

At length slow evening came:
They went with pitchers to the reedy brook ;
Lizzie most placid in her look,
Laura most like a leaping flame.
They drew the gurgling water from its deep ;
Lizzie plucked purple and rich golden flags,
Then turning homewards said : " The sunset flushes
Those furthest loftiest crags ;
Come, Laura, not another maiden lags,
No wilful squirrel wags,   30
The beasts and birds are fast asleep."
But Laura loitered still among the rushes
And said the bank was steep.

And said the hour was early still,
The dew not fall'n, the wind not chill :

Listening ever, but not catching
The customary cry,
" Come buy, come buy,"
With its iterated jingle
Of sugar-baited words :
Not for all her watching
Once discerning even one goblin
Racing, whisking, tumbling, hobbling ;
Let alone the herds
That used to tramp along the glen, 10
In groups or single,
Of brisk fruit-merchant men.

Till Lizzie urged, " O Laura, come ;
I hear the fruit-call, but I dare not look :
You should not loiter longer at this brook :
Come with me home.
The stars rise, the moon bends her arc,
Each glowworm winks her spark,
Let us get home before the night grows dark :
For clouds may gather 20
Though this is summer weather,
Put out the lights and drench us through ;
Then if we lost our way what should we do ? "

Laura turned cold as stone
To find her sister heard that cry alone,
That goblin cry,
" Come buy our fruits, come buy."
Must she then buy no more such dainty fruit ?
Must she no more such succous pasture find,
Gone deaf and blind ? 30
Her tree of life drooped from the root :
She said not one word in her heart's sore ache ;
But peering thro' the dimness, nought discerning,
Trudged home, her pitcher dripping all the way ;
So crept to bed, and lay

GOBLIN MARKET

Silent till Lizzie slept ;
Then sat up in a passionate yearning,
And gnashed her teeth for baulked desire, and wept
As if her heart would break.

Day after day, night after night,
Laura kept watch in vain
In sullen silence of exceeding pain.
She never caught again the goblin cry :
" Come buy, come buy " ;—
She never spied the goblin men
Hawking their fruits along the glen :
But when the noon waxed bright
Her hair grew thin and grey ;
She dwindled, as the fair full moon doth turn
To swift decay and burn
Her fire away.

One day remembering her kernel-stone
She set it by a wall that faced the south ;
Dewed it with tears, hoped for a root,
Watched for a waxing shoot, 20
But there came none ;
It never saw the sun,
It never felt the trickling moisture run :
While with sunk eyes and faded mouth
She dreamed of melons, as a traveller sees
False waves in desert drouth
With shade of leaf-crowned trees,
And burns the thirstier in the sandful breeze.

She no more swept the house,
Tended the fowls or cows, 30
Fetched honey, kneaded cakes of wheat,
Brought water from the brook :
But sat down listless in the chimney-nook
And would not eat.

POEMS OLD AND NEW

Tender Lizzie could not bear
To watch her sister's cankerous care
Yet not to share.
She night and morning
Caught the goblins' cry :
" Come buy our orchard fruits,
Come buy, come buy " :—
Beside the brook, along the glen,
She heard the tramp of goblin men,
The voice and stir
Poor Laura could not hear ;
Longed to buy fruit to comfort her,
But feared to pay too dear.
She thought of Jeanie in her grave,
Who should have been a bride ;
But who for joys brides hope to have
Fell sick and died
In her gay prime,
In earliest Winter time,
With the first glazing rime,
With the first snow-fall of crisp Winter time.

Till Laura dwindling
Seemed knocking at Death's door :
Then Lizzie weighed no more
Better and worse ;
But put a silver penny in her purse,
Kissed Laura, crossed the heath with clumps of furze
At twilight, halted by the brook :
And for the first time in her life
Began to listen and look.

Laughed every goblin
When they spied her peeping :
Came towards her hobbling,
Flying, running, leaping,

GOBLIN MARKET

Puffing and blowing,
Chuckling, clapping, crowing,
Clucking and gobbling,
Mopping and mowing,
Full of airs and graces,
Pulling wry faces,
Demure grimaces,
Cat-like and rat-like,
Ratel- and wombat-like,
Snail-paced in a hurry,   10
Parrot-voiced and whistler,
Helter skelter, hurry skurry,
Chattering like magpies,
Fluttering like pigeons,
Gliding like fishes,—
Hugged her and kissed her :
Squeezed and caressed her :
Stretched up their dishes,
Panniers, and plates :
" Look at our apples   20
Russet and dun,
Bob at our cherries,
Bite at our peaches,
Citrons and dates,
Grapes for the asking,
Pears red with basking
Out in the sun,
Plums on their twigs ;
Pluck them and suck them,
Pomegranates, figs."—   30

" Good folk," said Lizzie,
Mindful of Jeanie :
" Give me much and many " :—
Held out her apron,
Tossed them her penny.
" Nay, take a seat with us,

77

Honour and eat with us,"
They answered grinning :
" Our feast is but beginning.
Night yet is early,
Warm and dew-pearly,
Wakeful and starry :
Such fruits as these
No man can carry ;
Half their bloom would fly,
Half their dew would dry, 10
Half their flavour would pass by.
Sit down and feast with us,
Be welcome guest with us,
Cheer you and rest with us."—
" Thank you," said Lizzie : " But one waits
At home alone for me :
So without further parleying,
If you will not sell me any
Of your fruits though much and many,
Give me back my silver penny 20
I tossed you for a fee."—
They began to scratch their pates,
No longer wagging, purring,
But visibly demurring,
Grunting and snarling.
One called her proud,
Cross-grained, uncivil ;
Their tones waxed loud,
Their looks were evil.
Lashing their tails 30
They trod and hustled her,
Elbowed and jostled her,
Clawed with their nails,
Barking, mewing, hissing, mocking,
Tore her gown and soiled her stocking,
Twitched her hair out by the roots,
Stamped upon her tender feet,

GOBLIN MARKET

Held her hands and squeezed their fruits
Against her mouth to make her eat.

White and golden Lizzie stood,
Like a lily in a flood,—
Like a rock of blue-veined stone
Lashed by tides obstreperously,—
Like a beacon left alone
In a hoary roaring sea,
Sending up a golden fire,—
Like a fruit-crowned orange-tree   10
White with blossoms honey-sweet
Sore beset by wasp and bee,—
Like a royal virgin town
Topped with gilded dome and spire
Close beleaguered by a fleet
Mad to tug her standard down.

One may lead a horse to water,
Twenty cannot make him drink.
Though the goblins cuffed and caught her,
Coaxed and fought her,   20
Bullied and besought her,
Scratched her, pinched her black as ink,
Kicked and knocked her,
Mauled and mocked her,
Lizzie uttered not a word ;
Would not open lip from lip
Lest they should cram a mouthful in :
But laughed in heart to feel the drip
Of juice that syrupped all her face,
And lodged in dimples of her chin,   30
And streaked her neck which quaked like curd.
At last the evil people
Worn out by her resistance
Flung back her penny, kicked their fruit
Along whichever road they took,

Not leaving root or stone or shoot ;
Some writhed into the ground,
Some dived into the brook
With ring and ripple,
Some scudded on the gale without a sound,
Some vanished in the distance.

 In a smart, ache, tingle,
Lizzie went her way ;
Knew not was it night or day ;
Sprang up the bank, tore thro' the furze,   10
Threaded copse and dingle,
And heard her penny jingle
Bouncing in her purse,—
Its bounce was music to her ear.
She ran and ran
As if she feared some goblin man
Dogged her with gibe or curse
Or something worse :
But not one goblin skurried after,
Nor was she pricked by fear ;   20
The kind heart made her windy-paced
That urged her home quite out of breath with haste
And inward laughter.

 She cried " Laura," up the garden,
" Did you miss me ?
Come and kiss me.
Never mind my bruises,
Hug me, kiss me, suck my juices
Squeezed from goblin fruits for you,
Goblin pulp and goblin dew.   30
Eat me, drink me, love me ;
Laura, make much of me :
For your sake I have braved the glen
And had to do with goblin merchant men."

GOBLIN MARKET

Laura started from her chair,
Flung her arms up in the air,
Clutched her hair :
" Lizzie, Lizzie, have you tasted
For my sake the fruit forbidden ?
Must your light like mine be hidden,
Your young life like mine be wasted,
Undone in mine undoing
And ruined in my ruin,
Thirsty, cankered, goblin-ridden ? "—   10
She clung about her sister,
Kissed and kissed and kissed her :
Tears once again
Refreshed her shrunken eyes,
Dropping like rain
After long sultry drouth ;
Shaking with aguish fear, and pain,
She kissed and kissed her with a hungry mouth.

Her lips began to scorch,
That juice was wormwood to her tongue,   20
She loathed the feast :
Writhing as one possessed she leaped and sung,
Rent all her robe, and wrung
Her hands in lamentable haste,
And beat her breast.
Her locks streamed like the torch
Borne by a racer at full speed,
Or like the mane of horses in their flight,
Or like an eagle when she stems the light
Straight toward the sun,   30
Or like a caged thing freed,
Or like a flying flag when armies run.

Swift fire spread through her veins, knocked
    at her heart,
Met the fire smouldering there

And overbore its lesser flame ;
She gorged on bitterness without a name :
Ah ! fool, to choose such part
Of soul-consuming care !
Sense failed in the mortal strife :
Like the watch-tower of a town
Which an earthquake shatters down,
Like a lightning-stricken mast,
Like a wind-uprooted tree
Spun about,   10
Like a foam-topped waterspout
Cast down headlong in the sea,
She fell at last ;
Pleasure past and anguish past,
Is it death or is it life ?

   Life out of death.
That night long Lizzie watched by her,
Counted her pulse's flagging stir,
Felt for her breath,
Held water to her lips, and cooled her face   20
With tears and fanning leaves :
But when the first birds chirped about their
    eaves,
And early reapers plodded to the place
Of golden sheaves,
And dew-wet grass
Bowed in the morning winds so brisk to pass,
And new buds with new day
Opened of cup-like lilies on the stream,
Laura awoke as from a dream,
Laughed in the innocent old way,   30
Hugged Lizzie but not twice or thrice ;
Her gleaming locks showed not one thread of
    grey,
Her breath was sweet as May
And light danced in her eyes.

A RUNNABLE STAG

Days, weeks, months, years
Afterwards, when both were wives
With children of their own ;
Their mother-hearts beset with fears,
Their lives bound up in tender lives ;
Laura would call the little ones
And tell them of her early prime,
Those pleasant days long gone
Of not-returning time :
Would talk about the haunted glen,   10
The wicked, quaint fruit-merchant men,
Their fruits like honey to the throat
But poison in the blood ;
(Men sell not such in any town :)
Would tell them how her sister stood
In deadly peril to do her good,
And win the fiery antidote :
Then joining hands to little hands
Would bid them cling together,
" For there is no friend like a sister   20
In calm or stormy weather ;
To cheer one on the tedious way,
To fetch one if one goes astray,
To lift one if one totters down,
To strengthen whilst one stands."
    Christina Rossetti

A RUNNABLE STAG

When the pods went pop on the broom, green broom,
And apples began to be golden-skinned,
We harboured a stag in the Priory coomb,
And we feathered his trail up-wind, up-wind,
We feathered his trail up-wind—   30

POEMS OLD AND NEW

A stag of warrant, a stag, a stag,
A runnable stag, a kingly crop,
Brow, bay and tray and three on top,
A stag, a runnable stag.

Then the huntsman's horn rang yap, yap, yap,
  And " Forwards " we heard the harbourer shout ;
But 'twas only a brocket that broke a gap
  In the beechen underwood, driven out,
  From the underwood antlered out
    By warrant and might of the stag, the stag,   10
    The runnable stag, whose lordly mind
    Was bent on sleep, though beamed and tined
    He stood, a runnable stag.

So we tufted the covert till afternoon
  With Tinkerman's Pup and Bell-of-the-North ;
And hunters were sulky and hounds out of tune
  Before we tufted the right stag forth,
  Before we tufted him forth,
    The stag of warrant, the wily stag,
    The runnable stag with his kingly crop,   20
    Brow, bay and tray and three on top,
    The royal and runnable stag.

It was Bell-of-the-North and Tinkerman's Pup
  That stuck to the scent till the copse was drawn.
" Tally ho ! tally ho ! " and the hunt was up,
  The tufters whipped and the pack laid on,
  The resolute pack laid on,
    And the stag of warrant away at last,
    The runnable stag, the same, the same,
    His hoofs on fire, his horns like flame,   30
    A stag, a runnable stag.

" Let your gelding be : if you check or chide
  He stumbles at once and you're out of the hunt ;

A RUNNABLE STAG

For three hundred gentlemen, able to ride,
  On hunters accustomed to bear the brunt,
  Accustomed to bear the brunt,
    Are after the runnable stag, the stag,
    The runnable stag with his kingly crop,
    Brow, bay and tray and three on top,
    The right, the runnable stag."

By perilous paths in coomb and dell,
  The heather, the rocks, and the river-bed,
The pace grew hot, for the scent lay well,
  And a runnable stag goes right ahead,
  The quarry went right ahead—
    Ahead, ahead, and fast and far ;
    His antlered crest, his cloven hoof,
    Brow, bay and tray and three aloof,
    The stag, the runnable stag.

For a matter of twenty miles and more,
  By the densest hedge and the highest wall,
Through herds of bullocks he baffled the lore
  Of harbourer, huntsman, hounds and all,
  Of harbourer, hounds and all—
    The stag of warrant, the wily stag,
    For twenty miles, and five and five,
    He ran, and he never was caught alive,
    This stag, this runnable stag.

When he turned at bay in the leafy gloom,
  In the emerald gloom where the brook ran deep,
He heard in the distance the rollers boom,
  And he saw in a vision of peaceful sleep,
  In a wonderful vision of sleep,
    A stag of warrant, a stag, a stag,
    A runnable stag in a jewelled bed,
    Under the sheltering ocean dead,
    A stag, a runnable stag.

So a fateful hope lit up his eye,
And he opened his nostrils wide again,
And he tossed his branching antlers high
  As he headed the hunt down the Charlock glen,
  As he raced down the echoing glen
    For five miles more, the stag, the stag,
    For twenty miles, and five and five,
    Not to be caught now, dead or alive,
    The stag, the runnable stag.

Three hundred gentlemen, able to ride,   10
  Three hundred horses as gallant and free,
Beheld him escape on the evening tide,
  Far out till he sank in the Severn Sea,
  Till he sank in the depths of the sea—
    The stag, the buoyant stag, the stag
    That slept at last in a jewelled bed
    Under the sheltering ocean spread,
    The stag, the runnable stag.
                    JOHN DAVIDSON

HAWKE

IN seventeen hundred and fifty-nine,
  When Hawke came swooping from the West,   20
The French King's Admiral with twenty of the line,
  Was sailing forth, to sack us, out of Brest.
The ports of France were crowded, the quays of
      France a-hum
With thirty thousand soldiers marching to the drum,
For bragging time was over and fighting time was
      come
  When Hawke came swooping from the West.

'Twas long past noon of a wild November Day
  When Hawke came swooping from the West;

HE FELL AMONG THIEVES

He heard the breakers thundering in Quiberon Bay
But he flew the flag for battle, line abreast.
Down upon the quicksands roaring out of sight
Fiercely beat the storm-wind, darkly fell the night,
But they took the foe for pilot and the cannon's glare
    for light
When Hawke came swooping from the West.

The Frenchmen turned like a covey down the wind
When Hawke came swooping from the West ;
One he sank with all hands, one he caught and
    pinned,
And the shallows and the storm took the rest.   10
The guns that should have conquered us they rusted
    on the shore,
The men that would have mastered us they drummed
    and marched no more,
For England was England, and a mighty brood she
    bore
When Hawke came swooping from the West.
                     Sir Henry Newbolt

HE FELL AMONG THIEVES

" Ye have robbed," said he, " ye have slaughtered
    and made an end,
Take your ill-got plunder, and bury the dead :
What will ye more of your guest and sometime
    friend ? "
" Blood for our blood," they said.

He laughed : " If one may settle the score for five,
    I am ready ; but let the reckoning stand till
    day :   20
I have loved the sunlight as dearly as any alive."
    " You shall die at dawn," said they.

POEMS OLD AND NEW

He flung his empty revolver down the slope,
   He climbed alone to the Eastward edge of the trees;
All night long in a dream untroubled of hope
   He brooded, clasping his knees.

He did not hear the monotonous roar that fills
   The ravine where the Yassin river sullenly flows;
He did not see the starlight on the Laspur hills,
   Or the far Afghan snows.

He saw the April noon on his books aglow,
   The wistaria trailing in at the window wide;
He heard his father's voice from the terrace below
   Calling him down to ride.

He saw the gray little church across the park,
   The mounds that hide the loved and honoured dead;
The Norman arch, the chancel softly dark,
   The brasses black and red.

He saw the School Close, sunny and green,
   The runner beside him, the stand by the parapet wall,
The distant tape, and the crowd roaring between
   His own name over all.

He saw the dark wainscot and timbered roof,
   The long tables, and the faces merry and keen;
The College Eight and their trainer dining aloof,
   The Dons on the daïs serene.

He watched the liner's stem ploughing the foam,
   He felt her trembling speed and the thrash of her screw;
He heard her passengers' voices talking of home,
   He saw the flag she flew.

THE HIGHWAYMAN

And now it was dawn. He rose strong on his feet,
  And strode to his ruined camp below the wood;
He drank the breath of the morning cool and sweet;
  His murderers round him stood.

Light on the Laspur hills was broadening fast,
  The blood-red snow-peaks chilled to a dazzling white:
He turned, and saw the golden circle at last,
  Cut by the Eastern height.

" O glorious Life, who dwellest in earth and sun,
  I have lived, I praise and adore Thee."   10
                              A sword swept.
Over the pass the voices one by one
  Faded, and the hill slept.
                              SIR HENRY NEWBOLT

THE HIGHWAYMAN

PART I

THE wind was a torrent of darkness among the gusty trees,
The moon was a ghostly galleon tossed upon cloudy seas,
The road was a ribbon of moonlight over the purple moor,
And the highwayman came riding—
    Riding—riding,
The highwayman came riding, up to the old inn-door.

He'd a French cocked-hat on his forehead, a bunch of lace at his chin,   20
A coat of claret velvet, and breeches of brown doeskin,

They fitted with never a wrinkle ; his boots were up
    to the thigh ;
And he rode with a jewelled twinkle,
    His pistol butts a-twinkle,
His rapier hilt a-twinkle, under the jewelled sky.

Over the cobbles he clattered and clashed in the dark
    inn-yard ;
And he tapped with his whip on the shutters, but all
    was locked and barred ;
He whistled a tune to the window, and who should be
    waiting there
But the landlord's black-eyed daughter,
    Bess, the landlord's daughter,
Plaiting a dark red love-knot into her long black hair. 10

And dark in the dark old inn-yard a stable wicket
    creaked,
Where Tim the ostler listened ; his face was white
    and peaked ;
His eyes were hollows of madness, his hair like mouldy
    hay,
But he loved the landlord's daughter,
    The landlord's red-lipped daughter—
Dumb as a dog he listened, and he heard the robber
    say—

" One kiss, my bonnie sweetheart, I'm after a prize
    to-night,
But I shall be back with the yellow gold before the
    morning light ;
Yet, if they press me sharply, and harry me through
    the day,
Then look for me by moonlight,   20
    Watch for me by moonlight,
I'll come to thee by moonlight, though hell should
    bar the way."

THE HIGHWAYMAN

He rose upright in the stirrups ; he scarce could reach her hand,
But she loosened her hair i' the casement ! His face burnt like a brand
As the black cascade of perfume came tumbling over his breast ;
And he kissed the waves in the moonlight
    (Oh, sweet black waves in the moon-light) ;
Then he tugged at his rein in the moonlight, and galloped away to the west.

Part II

He did not come in the dawning ; he did not come at noon ;
And out o' the tawny sunset, before the rise o' the moon,
When the road was a gipsy's ribbon, looping the purple moor,
A red-coat troop came marching—   10
    Marching—marching,
King George's men came marching, up to the old inn-door.

They said no word to the landlord, they drank his ale instead,
But they gagged his daughter and bound her to the foot of her narrow bed ;
Two of them knelt at her casement, with muskets at their side !
There was death at every window ;
    And hell at one dark window ;
For Bess could see, through her casement, the road that he would ride.

They had tied her up to attention, with many a
    sniggering jest ;
They had bound a musket beside her, with the barrel
    beneath her breast !
" Now keep good watch ! " and they kissed her. She
    heard the dead man say—
Look for me by moonlight ;
    Watch for me by moonlight ;
*I'll come to thee by moonlight, though hell should bar the
    way !*

She twisted her hands behind her ; but all the knots
    held good !
She writhed her hands till her fingers were wet with
    sweat, or blood,
They stretched and strained in the darkness, and the
    hours crawled by like years,
Till, now, on the stroke of midnight,   10
    Cold, on the stroke of midnight,
The tip of one finger touched it ! The trigger at least
    was hers !

The tip of one finger touched it ; she strove no more
    for the rest !
Up, she stood up to attention, with the barrel beneath
    her breast,
She would not risk their hearing ; she would not strive
    again ;
For the road lay bare in the moonlight ;
    Blank and bare in the moonlight ;
And the blood of her veins in the moonlight throbbed
    to her love's refrain.

Tlot-tlot ; tlot-tlot ! Had they heard it ? The horse-
    hoofs ringing clear ;
Tlot-tlot, tlot-tlot, in the distance ! Were they deaf that
    they did not hear ?   20

THE HIGHWAYMAN

Down the ribbon of moonlight, over the brow of the hill,
The highwayman came riding,
    Riding, riding !
The red-coats looked to their priming ! she stood up,
straight and still !

Tlot-tlot, in the frosty silence ! *Tlot-tlot*, in the echoing night !
Nearer he came and nearer ! Her face was like a light !
Her eyes grew wide for a moment ; she drew one last deep breath,
Then her finger moved in the moonlight,
    Her musket shattered the moonlight,
Shattered her breast in the moonlight, and warned him—with her death.   10

He turned ; he spurred to the Westward ; he did not know who stood
Bowed, with her head o'er the musket, drenched with her own red blood !
Not till the dawn he heard it, and slowly blanched to hear
How Bess, the landlord's daughter,
    The landlord's black-eyed daughter,
Had watched for her love in the moonlight, and died in the darkness there.

Back, he spurred like a madman, shrieking a curse to the sky,
With the white road smoking behind him and his rapier brandished high !
Blood-red were his spurs i' the golden noon ; wine-red was his velvet coat ;
When they shot him down on the highway,   20
    Down like a dog on the highway :
And he lay in his blood on the highway, with the bunch of lace at his throat.

POEMS OLD AND NEW

. . . . . .

*And still of a winter's night, they say, when the wind is in
    the trees,
When the moon is a ghostly galleon tossed upon cloudy seas,
When the road is a ribbon of moonlight over the purple moor,
A highwayman comes riding—
        Riding—riding,
A highwayman comes riding, up to the old inn-door.*

*Over the cobbles he clatters and clangs in the dark inn-yard;
And he taps with his whip on the shutters, but all is locked
    and barred;
He whistles a tune to the window, and who should be
    waiting there
But the landlord's black-eyed daughter,* 10
        *Bess, the landlord's daughter,
Plaiting a dark red love-knot into her long black hair.*
                                            ALFRED NOYES

LYRICAL AND DESCRIPTIVE POEMS

THE PASSIONATE SHEPHERD TO HIS LOVE

Come live with me and be my Love,
And we will all the pleasures prove
That hills and valleys, dale and field,
And all the craggy mountains yield.

There will we sit upon the rocks
And see the shepherds feed their flocks,
By shallow rivers, to whose falls
Melodious birds sing madrigals.

There will I make thee beds of roses
And a thousand fragrant posies,   10
A cap of flowers, and a kirtle
Embroider'd all with leaves of myrtle.

A gown made of the finest wool,
Which from our pretty lambs we pull,
Fair linèd slippers for the cold,
With buckles of the purest gold.

A belt of straw and ivy buds
With coral clasps and amber studs :
And if these pleasures may thee move,
Come live with me and be my Love.   20

Thy silver dishes for thy meat
As precious as the gods do eat,
Shall on an ivory table be
Prepared each day for thee and me.

The shepherd swains shall dance and sing
For thy delight each May-morning :
If these delights thy mind may move,
Then live with me and be my Love.
     CHRISTOPHER MARLOWE

WINTER

WHEN icicles hang by the wall,
 And Dick the shepherd blows his nail,
And Tom bears logs into the hall,
 And milk comes frozen home in pail,
When blood is nipp'd and ways be foul,
Then nightly sings the staring owl,   10
 To-whit !
To-who !—a merry note,
While greasy Joan doth keel the pot.

When all aloud the wind doth blow,
 And coughing drowns the parson's saw,
And birds sit brooding in the snow,
 And Marian's nose looks red and raw,
When roasted crabs hiss in the bowl,
Then nightly sings the staring owl,
 To-whit !   20
To-who !—a merry note,
While greasy Joan doth keel the pot.
     WILLIAM SHAKESPEARE

FIDELE

FEAR no more the heat o' the sun,
 Nor the furious winter's rages ;
Thou thy worldly task hast done,
 Home art gone, and ta'en thy wages :

CHARACTER OF A HAPPY LIFE

Golden lads and girls all must,
As chimney-sweepers, come to dust.

Fear no more the frown o' the great,
  Thou art past the tyrant's stroke ;
Care no more to clothe and eat ;
  To thee the reed is as the oak :
The sceptre, learning, physic, must
All follow this, and come to dust.

Fear no more the lightning-flash,
  Nor the all-dreaded thunder-stone ;   10
Fear not slander, censure rash ;
  Thou hast finish'd joy and moan :
All lovers young, all lovers must
Consign to thee, and come to dust.
               WILLIAM SHAKESPEARE

CHARACTER OF A HAPPY LIFE

How happy is he born or taught
  That serveth not another's will ;
Whose armour is his honest thought,
  And silly truth his highest skill !

Whose passions not his masters are,
  Whose soul is still prepared for death ; 20
Untied unto the world with care
  Of princely love or vulgar breath ;

Who hath his life from rumours freed,
  Whose conscience is his strong retreat ;
Whose state can neither flatterers feed,
  Nor ruin make accusers great ;

POEMS OLD AND NEW

Who envieth none whom chance doth raise
  Or vice ; who never understood
How deepest wounds are given with praise ;
  Nor rules of state, but rules of good :

Who God doth late and early pray
  More of his grace than gifts to lend ;
Who entertains the harmless day
  With a well-chosen book or friend ;

—This man is free from servile bands
  Of hope to rise, or fear to fall ;   10
Lord of himself, though not of lands ;
  And having nothing, he hath all.
             Sir Henry Wotton

TO CELIA

Drink to me only with thine eyes,
  And I will pledge with mine ;
Or leave a kiss but in the cup,
  And I'll not look for wine.
The thirst that from the soul doth rise,
  Doth ask a drink divine :
But might I of Jove's nectar sup,
  I would not change for thine.   20

I sent thee late a rosy wreath,
  Not so much honouring thee,
As giving it a hope that there
  It could not withered be.
But thou thereon didst only breathe,
  And sent'st it back to me :
Since when it grows, and smells, I swear,
  Not of itself, but thee.
             Ben Jonson

THE VILLAGE PREACHER

HYMN TO DIANA

QUEEN and huntress, chaste and fair,
  Now the sun is laid to sleep,
Seated in thy silver chair,
  State in wonted manner keep :
    Hesperus entreats thy light,
    Goddess excellently bright.

Earth, let not thy envious shade
  Dare itself to interpose ;
Cynthia's shining orb was made
  Heaven to clear when day did close :   10
    Bless us then with wishèd sight,
    Goddess excellently bright.

Lay thy bow of pearl apart,
  And thy crystal-shining quiver ;
Give unto the flying hart
  Space to breathe, how short soever :
    Thou that mak'st a day of night—
    Goddess excellently bright.
                  BEN JONSON

THE VILLAGE PREACHER

NEAR yonder copse, where once the garden smiled,
And still where many a garden flower grows wild ; 20
There, where a few torn shrubs the place disclose,
The village preacher's modest mansion rose.
A man he was to all the country dear,
And passing rich with forty pounds a year ;
Remote from towns he ran his godly race,
Nor e'er had changed, nor wished to change, his place ;

Unpractised he to fawn, or seek for power,
By doctrines fashioned to the varying hour ;
Far other aims his heart had learned to prize,
More skilled to raise the wretched than to rise.
His house was known to all the vagrant train,
He chid their wanderings, but relieved their pain ;
The long-remembered beggar was his guest,
Whose beard descending swept his agèd breast ;
The ruined spendthrift, now no longer proud,
Claimed kindred there, and had his claims allowed ;
The broken soldier, kindly bade to stay,   11
Sat by his fire, and talked the night away,
Wept o'er his wounds, or, tales of sorrow done,
Shouldered his crutch and showed how fields were won.
Pleased with his guests, the good man learned to glow,
And quite forgot their vices in their woe ;
Careless their merits or their faults to scan,
His pity gave ere charity began.
  Thus to relieve the wretched was his pride,
And e'en his failings leaned to Virtue's side ;   20
But in his duty, prompt at every call,
He watched and wept, he prayed and felt, for all ;
And, as a bird each fond endearment tries
To tempt its new-fledged offspring to the skies,
He tried each art, reproved each dull delay,
Allured to brighter worlds, and led the way.
  Beside the bed where parting life was laid,
And sorrow, guilt, and pain, by turns dismayed,
The reverend champion stood. At his control
Despair and anguish fled the struggling soul ;   30
Comfort came down the trembling wretch to raise,
And his last faltering accents whispered praise.
  At church, with meek and unaffected grace,
His looks adorned the venerable place ;

THE VILLAGE SCHOOLMASTER

Truth from his lips prevailed with double sway,
And fools, who came to scoff, remained to pray.
The service past, around the pious man,
With steady zeal, each honest rustic ran ;
Even children followed, with endearing wile,
And plucked his gown, to share the good man's smile ;
His ready smile a parent's warmth expressed,
Their welfare pleased him, and their cares distressed ;
To them his heart, his love, his griefs were given,
But all his serious thoughts had rest in heaven. 10
As some tall cliff that lifts its awful form,
Swells from the vale, and midway leaves the storm,
Though round its breast the rolling clouds are spread
Eternal sunshine settles on its head.

OLIVER GOLDSMITH

THE VILLAGE SCHOOLMASTER

BESIDE yon straggling fence that skirts the way,
With blossomed furze unprofitably gay,
There, in his noisy mansion, skilled to rule,
The village master taught his little school ;
A man severe he was, and stern to view ;
I knew him well, and every truant knew ; 20
Well had the boding tremblers learned to trace
The day's disasters in his morning face ;
Full well they laughed with counterfeited glee
At all his jokes, for many a joke had he ;
Full well the busy whisper, circling round,
Conveyed the dismal tidings when he frowned :
Yet he was kind ; or if severe in aught,
The love he bore to learning was in fault.
The village all declared how much he knew ;
'Twas certain he could write and cypher too ; 30
Lands he could measure, terms and tides presage,
And e'en the story ran that he could gauge.

POEMS OLD AND NEW

In arguing, too, the parson owned his skill,
For e'en though vanquished, he could argue still;
While words of learned length and thund'ring sound
Amazed the gazing rustics ranged around,
And still they gazed, and still the wonder grew
That one small head could carry all he knew.
But past is all his fame. The very spot,
Where many a time he triumphed, is forgot.
OLIVER GOLDSMITH

THE TIGER

TIGER! Tiger! burning bright
In the forests of the night,   10
What immortal hand or eye
Could frame thy fearful symmetry?

In what distant deeps or skies
Burnt the fire of thine eyes?
On what wings dare he aspire?
What the hand dare seize the fire?

And what shoulder, and what art,
Could twist the sinews of thy heart?
And, when thy heart began to beat,
What dread hand forgèd thy dread feet?   20

What the hammer? what the chain?
In what furnace was thy brain?
What the anvil? what dread grasp
Dare its deadly terrors clasp?

When the stars threw down their spears,
And water'd heaven with their tears,
Did he smile his work to see?
Did he who made the Lamb make thee?

THE SOLITARY REAPER

Tiger ! Tiger ! burning bright
In the forests of the night,
What immortal hand or eye
Dare frame thy fearful symmetry ?
　　　　　　　　　WILLIAM BLAKE

THE SOLITARY REAPER

BEHOLD her, single in the field,
　Yon solitary Highland Lass !
Reaping and singing by herself ;
　Stop here, or gently pass !
Alone she cuts and binds the grain,
And sings a melancholy strain ;　　　　10
O listen ! for the Vale profound
Is overflowing with the sound.

No Nightingale did ever chaunt
　More welcome notes to weary bands
Of travellers in some shady haunt,
　Among Arabian sands :
A voice so thrilling ne'er was heard
In spring-time from the Cuckoo-bird,
Breaking the silence of the seas
Among the farthest Hebrides.　　　　20

Will no one tell me what she sings ?—
　Perhaps the plaintive numbers flow
For old, unhappy, far-off things,
　And battles long ago :
Or is it some more humble lay,
Familiar matter of to-day ?
Some natural sorrow, loss, or pain,
That has been, and may be again ?

Whate'er the theme, the Maiden sang
   As if her song could have no ending ;
I saw her singing at her work,
   And o'er the sickle bending ;—
I listen'd, motionless and still ;
And, as I mounted up the hill,
The music in my heart I bore,
Long after it was heard no more.
               WILLIAM WORDSWORTH

UPON WESTMINSTER BRIDGE

EARTH has not anything to show more fair ;
Dull would he be of soul who could pass by   10
A sight so touching in its majesty :
The City now doth like a garment wear
The beauty of the morning ; silent, bare,
Ships, towers, domes, theatres, and temples lie
Open unto the fields and to the sky ;
All bright and glittering in the smokeless air.
Never did sun more beautifully steep
In his first splendour, valley, rock, or hill ;
Ne'er saw I, never felt, a calm so deep !
The river glideth at his own sweet will ;   20
Dear God ! the very houses seem asleep ;
And all that mighty heart is lying still !
               WILLIAM WORDSWORTH

SHE DWELT AMONG THE UNTRODDEN WAYS

SHE dwelt among the untrodden ways
   Beside the springs of Dove,
A Maid whom there were none to praise
   And very few to love :

SOLDIER, REST!

A violet by a mossy stone
  Half hidden from the eye!
—Fair as a star, when only one
  Is shining in the sky.

She lived unknown, and few could know
  When Lucy ceased to be;
But she is in her grave, and oh,
  The difference to me!
                    WILLIAM WORDSWORTH

LULLABY OF AN INFANT CHIEF

O, HUSH thee, my baby, thy sire was a knight,
Thy mother a lady both lovely and bright; 10
The woods and the glens, from the tower which we see,
They all are belonging, dear baby, to thee.

O, fear not the bugle, though loudly it blows,
It calls but the warders that guard thy repose;
Their bows would be bended, their blades would be red,
Ere the step of a foeman drew near to thy bed.

O, hush thee, my baby, the time will soon come
When thy sleep shall be broken by trumpet and drum;
Then hush thee, my darling, take rest while you may,
For strife comes with manhood, and waking with day. 20
                    SIR WALTER SCOTT

SOLDIER, REST!

SOLDIER, rest! thy warfare o'er,
  Sleep the sleep that knows not breaking;
Dream of battled fields no more,
  Days of danger, nights of waking.

POEMS OLD AND NEW

In our isle's enchanted hall
    Hands unseen thy couch are strewing,
Fairy strains of music fall,
    Every sense in slumber dewing.
Soldier, rest ! thy warfare o'er,
Dream of fighting fields no more :
Sleep the sleep that knows not breaking,
Morn of toil, nor night of waking.

No rude sound shall reach thine ear,
    Armour's clang, or war-steed champing,   10
Trump nor pibroch summon here
    Mustering clan, or squadron tramping.
Yet the lark's shrill fife may come
    At the daybreak from the fallow,
And the bittern sound his drum,
    Booming from the sedgy shallow.
Ruder sounds shall none be near,
Guards nor warders challenge here,
Here's no war-steed's neigh and champing,
Shouting clans or squadrons stamping.   20

Huntsman, rest ! thy chase is done ;
    While our slumbrous spells assail ye,
Dream not, with the rising sun,
    Bugles here shall sound reveillé.
Sleep ! the deer is in his den ;
    Sleep ! thy hounds are by thee lying ;
Sleep ! nor dream in yonder glen,
    How thy gallant steed lay dying.
Huntsman, rest ! thy chase is done,
Think not of the rising sun,   30
For at dawning to assail ye,
Here no bugles sound reveillé.
                SIR WALTER SCOTT

PIBROCH OF DONUIL DHU

CORONACH

He is gone on the mountain,
    He is lost to the forest,
Like a summer-dried fountain,
    When our need was the sorest.
The font, reappearing,
    From the raindrops shall borrow,
But to us comes no cheering,
    To Duncan no morrow !

The hand of the reaper
    Takes the ears that are hoary,   10
But the voice of the weeper
    Wails manhood in glory.
The autumn winds rushing
    Waft the leaves that are searest,
But our flower was in flushing,
    When blighting was nearest.

Fleet foot on the correi,
    Sage counsel in cumber,
Red hand in the foray,
    How sound is thy slumber !   20
Like the dew on the mountain,
    Like the foam on the river,
Like the bubble on the fountain,
    Thou art gone, and for ever !
              Sir Walter Scott

PIBROCH OF DONUIL DHU

Pibroch of Donuil Dhu,
    Pibroch of Donuil,
Wake thy wild voice anew,
    Summon Clan-Conuil.

POEMS OLD AND NEW

Come away, come away,
  Hark to the summons !
Come in your war array,
  Gentles and commons.

Come from deep glen, and
  From mountain so rocky,
The war-pipe and pennon
  Are at Inverlochy.
Come every hill-plaid, and
  True heart that wears one,
Come every steel blade, and
  Strong hand that bears one.

Leave untended the herd,
  The flock without shelter ;
Leave the corpse uninterr'd,
  The bride at the altar ;
Leave the deer, leave the steer,
  Leave nets and barges :
Come with your fighting gear,
  Broadswords and targes.

Come as the winds come, when
  Forests are rended,
Come as the waves come, when
  Navies are stranded :
Faster come, faster come,
  Faster and faster,
Chief, vassal, page and groom,
  Tenant and master.

Fast they come, fast they come ;
  See how they gather !
Wide waves the eagle plume,
  Blended with heather.

KUBLA KHAN

Cast your plaids, draw your blades,
Forward, each man, set !
Pibroch of Donuil Dhu,
Knell for the onset !
                    SIR WALTER SCOTT

KUBLA KHAN

IN Xanadu did Kubla Khan
  A stately pleasure-dome decree :
Where Alph, the sacred river, ran
Through caverns measureless to man
  Down to a sunless sea.
So twice five miles of fertile ground   10
With walls and towers were girdled round :
And there were gardens bright with sinuous rills,
Where blossomed many an incense-bearing tree ;
And here were forests ancient as the hills,
Enfolding sunny spots of greenery.

But oh, that deep romantic chasm which slanted
Down the green hill athwart a cedarn cover !
A savage place ! as holy and enchanted
As e'er beneath a waning moon was haunted
By woman wailing for her demon-lover !   20
And from this chasm, with ceaseless turmoil seething,
As if this earth in fast thick pants were breathing,
A mighty fountain momently was forced ;
Amid whose swift half-intermitted burst
Huge fragments vaulted like rebounding hail,
Or chaffy grain beneath the thresher's flail :
And 'mid these dancing rocks at once and ever
It flung up momently the sacred river.
Five miles meandering with a mazy motion
Through wood and dale the sacred river ran,   30
Then reach'd the caverns measureless to man,
And sank in tumult to a lifeless ocean :

And 'mid this tumult Kubla heard from far
Ancestral voices prophesying war !

    The shadow of the dome of pleasure
      Floated midway on the waves ;
    Where was heard the mingled measure
      From the fountain and the caves.
It was a miracle of rare device,
A sunny pleasure-dome with caves of ice !

    A damsel with a dulcimer
      In a vision once I saw :
    It was an Abyssinian maid,
      And on her dulcimer she play'd,
    Singing of Mount Abora.
    Could I revive within me
      Her symphony and song,
To such a deep delight 'twould win me,
That with music loud and long
I would build that dome in air,
That sunny dome ! those caves of ice !
And all who heard should see them there,
And all should cry, Beware ! Beware !
His flashing eyes, his floating hair !
Weave a circle round him thrice,
    And close your eyes with holy dread,
    For he on honey-dew hath fed,
And drunk the milk of Paradise.
          SAMUEL TAYLOR COLERIDGE

THE PARROT

A PARROT from the Spanish main,
    Full young and early caged, came o'er,
    With bright wings, to the bleak domain
      Of Mullah's shore.

SHE WALKS IN BEAUTY

To spicy groves where he had wọn
   His plumage of resplendent hue,
His native fruits, and skies, and sun,
   He bade adieu.

For these he changed the smoke of turf,
   A heathery land and misty sky,
And turned on rocks and raging surf
   His golden eye.

But petted in our climate cold,
   He lived and chattered many a day: 10
Until with age, from green and gold
   His wings grew grey.

At last when blind, and seeming dumb,
   He scolded, laugh'd, and spoke no more,
A Spanish stranger chanced to come
   To Mullah's shore;

He hail'd the bird in Spanish speech,
   The bird in Spanish speech replied;
Flapp'd round the cage with joyous screech,
   Dropt down, and died.   20
              THOMAS CAMPBELL

SHE WALKS IN BEAUTY

SHE walks in beauty, like the night
   Of cloudless climes and starry skies,
And all that's best of dark and bright
   Meet in her aspect and her eyes,
Thus mellow'd to that tender light
   Which heaven to gaudy day denies.

One shade the more, one ray the less,
   Had half impair'd the nameless grace
Which waves in every raven tress,
   Or softly lightens o'er her face,
Where thoughts serenely sweet express
   How pure, how dear their dwelling-place.

And on that cheek and o'er that brow
   So soft, so calm, yet eloquent,
The smiles that win, the tints that glow
   But tell of days in goodness spent,   10
A mind at peace with all below,
   A heart whose love is innocent.
                              LORD BYRON

TO NIGHT

SWIFTLY walk over the western wave,
         Spirit of Night !
Out of the misty eastern cave,
   Where, all the long and lone daylight,
Thou wovest dreams of joy and fear
Which make thee terrible and dear,—
         Swift be thy flight !

Wrap thy form in a mantle grey,   20
         Star-inwrought !
Blind with thine hair the eyes of Day,
   Kiss her until she be wearied out,
Then wander o'er city, and sea, and land,
Touching all with thine opiate wand—
         Come, long-sought !

When I arose and saw the dawn,
         I sigh'd for thee ;
When light rode high, and the dew was gone,

THE HUMAN SEASONS

And noon lay heavy on flower and tree,
And the weary Day turn'd to his rest,
Lingering like an unloved guest,
    I sigh'd for thee.

Thy brother Death came, and cried,
    " Wouldst thou me ? "
Thy sweet child Sleep, the filmy-eyed,
    Murmur'd like a noontide bee,
" Shall I nestle near thy side ?
Wouldst thou me ? "—And I replied,   10
    " No, not thee ! "

Death will come when thou art dead,
    Soon, too soon—
Sleep will come when thou art fled ;
    Of neither would I ask the boon
I ask of thee, belovèd Night—
Swift be thine approaching flight,
    Come soon, soon !
        PERCY BYSSHE SHELLEY

THE HUMAN SEASONS

FOUR seasons fill the measure of the year ;
  There are four seasons in the mind of man :   20
He has his lusty Spring, when fancy clear
  Takes in all beauty with an easy span :
He has his Summer, when luxuriously
  Spring's honey'd cud of youthful thought he loves
To ruminate, and by such dreaming high
  Is nearest unto heaven : quiet coves

POEMS OLD AND NEW

His soul has in its Autumn, when his wings
He furleth close ; contented so to look
On mists in idleness—to let fair things
Pass by unheeded as a threshold brook.
He has his Winter too of pale misfeature,
Or else he would forgo his mortal nature.
JOHN KEATS

ON FIRST LOOKING INTO CHAPMAN'S HOMER

MUCH have I travell'd in the realms of gold,
  And many goodly states and kingdoms seen ;
  Round many western islands have I been
Which bards in fealty to Apollo hold. 10
Oft of one wide expanse had I been told
  That deep-brow'd Homer ruled as his demesne ;
  Yet did I never breathe its pure serene
Till I heard Chapman speak out loud and bold :
Then felt I like some watcher of the skies
  When a new planet swims into his ken ;
Or like stout Cortez, when with eagle eyes
  He stared at the Pacific—and all his men
Look'd at each other with a wild surmise—
  Silent, upon a peak in Darien. 20
JOHN KEATS

TO AUTUMN

Season of mists and mellow fruitfulness !
Close bosom-friend of the maturing sun ;
Conspiring with him how to load and bless
  With fruit the vines that round the thatch-eaves run;
To bend with apples the moss'd cottage-trees,
  And fill all fruit with ripeness to the core ;
    To swell the gourd, and plump the hazel shells
With a sweet kernel ; to set budding more,
And still more, later flowers for the bees,
Until they think warm days will never cease,   10
    For Summer has o'er-brimm'd their clammy cells.

Who hath not seen thee oft amid thy store ?
  Sometimes whoever seeks abroad may find
Thee sitting careless on a granary floor,
  Thy hair soft-lifted by the winnowing wind ;
Or on a half-reap'd furrow sound asleep,
  Drowsed with the fume of poppies, while thy hook
    Spares the next swath and all its twinèd flowers;
And sometimes like a gleaner thou dost keep
  Steady thy laden head across a brook ;   20
  Or by a cider-press, with patient look,
    Thou watchest the last oozings, hours by hours.

Where are the songs of Spring ? Ay, where are they ?
  Think not of them, thou hast thy music too,—
While barrèd clouds bloom the soft-dying day,
  And touch the stubble-plains with rosy hue ;
Then in a wailful choir the small gnats mourn
  Among the river sallows, borne aloft
    Or sinking as the light wind lives or dies ;

And full-grown lambs loud bleat from hilly bourn ;
Hedge-crickets sing ; and now with treble soft
The redbreast whistles from a garden-croft ;
And gathering swallows twitter in the skies.
JOHN KEATS

AUTUMN

I LOVE the fitful gust that shakes
    The casement all the day,
And from the glossy elm tree takes
    The faded leaves away,
Twirling them by the window pane
With thousand others down the lane.

I love to see the shaking twig
    Dance till the shut of eve,
The sparrow on the cottage rig,
    Whose chirp would make believe
That Spring was just now flirting by
In Summer's lap with flowers to lie.

I love to see the cottage smoke
    Curl upwards through the trees,
The pigeons nestled round the cote
    On November days like these ;
The cock upon the dunghill crowing,
The mill sails on the heath a-going.

The feather from the raven's breast
    Falls on the stubble lea,
The acorns near the old crow's nest
    Drop pattering down the tree ;
The grunting pigs, that wait for all,
Scramble and hurry where they fall.
JOHN CLARE

BLOW, BUGLE, BLOW

THE EAGLE

HE clasps the crag with crooked hands ;
Close to the sun in lonely lands,
Ring'd with the azure world, he stands.

The wrinkled sea beneath him crawls ;
He watches from his mountain walls,
And like a thunderbolt he falls.
LORD TENNYSON

BLOW, BUGLE, BLOW

THE splendour falls on castle walls
  And snowy summits old in story :
The long light shakes across the lakes,
  And the wild cataract leaps in glory. 10
Blow, bugle, blow, set the wild echoes flying,
Blow, bugle ; answer, echoes, dying, dying, dying.

O hark, O hear ! how thin and clear,
  And thinner, clearer, farther going !
O sweet and far from cliff and scar
  The horns of Elfland faintly blowing !
Blow, let us hear the purple glens replying :
Blow, bugle ; answer, echoes, dying, dying, dying.

O love, they die in yon rich sky,
  They faint on hill or field or river : 20
Our echoes roll from soul to soul,
  And grow for ever and for ever.
Blow, bugle, blow, set the wild echoes flying,
And answer, echoes, answer, dying, dying, dying.
LORD TENNYSON

POEMS OLD AND NEW

HOME-THOUGHTS, FROM ABROAD

Oh, to be in England
Now that April's there,
And whoever wakes in England
Sees, some morning, unaware,
That the lowest boughs and the brushwood sheaf
Round the elm-tree bole are in tiny leaf,
While the chaffinch sings on the orchard bough
In England—now!

And after April, when May follows,
And the whitethroat builds, and all the swallows!　10
Hark, where my blossomed pear-tree in the hedge
Leans to the field and scatters on the clover
Blossoms and dewdrops—at the bent spray's edge—
That's the wise thrush; he sings each song twice over,
Lest you should think he never could recapture
The first fine careless rapture!
And though the fields look rough with hoary dew,
All will be gay when noontide wakes anew
The buttercups, the little children's dower
—Far brighter than this gaudy melon-flower!　20
　　　　　　　　ROBERT BROWNING

O CAPTAIN! MY CAPTAIN!

O Captain! my Captain! our fearful trip is done,
The ship has weather'd every rack, the prize we
　　sought is won,
The port is near, the bells I hear, the people all
　　exulting,
While follow eyes the steady keel, the vessel grim
　　and daring;

THE SCHOLAR GIPSY

But O heart ! heart ! heart !
   O the bleeding drops of red !
     Where on the deck my Captain lies,
       Fallen cold and dead.

O Captain ! my Captain ! rise up and hear the bells ;
Rise up—for you the flag is flung—for you the bugle trills,
For you bouquets and ribbon'd wreaths—for you the shores a-crowding,
For you they call, the swaying mass, their eager faces turning ;
   Here, Captain ! dear father !
     This arm beneath your head !   10
      It is some dream that on the deck
       You've fallen cold and dead.

My Captain does not answer, his lips are pale and still,
My father does not feel my arm, he has no pulse nor will ;
The ship is anchor'd safe and sound, its voyage closed and done,
From fearful trip the victor ship comes in with object won ;
   Exult, O shores ! and ring, O bells !
     But I, with mournful tread,
      Walk the deck my Captain lies,
       Fallen cold and dead.   20
                    WALT WHITMAN

THE SCHOLAR GIPSY

[There was very lately a lad in the University of Oxford, who was by his poverty forced to leave his studies there ; and at last to join himself to a company of vagabond gipsies. Among these extravagant people, by the insinuating subtilty of his carriage, he quickly got so much of their love and esteem as that they discovered to him their mystery. After he had been a pretty while well exercised in the trade, there chanced to ride by a couple of scholars, who had formerly been of his acquaintance. They quickly spied out their old friend among the gipsies; and he gave them an account of the necessity which drove him to that kind of life, and told them that the people he went with were not such impostors as they were taken for, but that they had a traditional kind of learning among them, and could do wonders by the power of imagination, their fancy binding that of others: that himself had learned much of their art, and when he had compassed the whole secret, he intended, he said, to leave their company, and give the world an account of what he had learned.—GLANVIL's *Vanity of Dogmatizing*, 1661.]

Go, for they call you, shepherd, from the hill;
  Go, shepherd, and untie the wattled cotes!
    No longer leave thy wistful flock unfed,
    Nor let thy bawling fellows rack their throats,
  Nor the cropp'd herbage shoot another head.
    But when the fields are still,
  And the tired men and dogs all gone to rest,
    And only the white sheep are sometimes seen
    Cross and recross the strips of moon-blanch'd green,
  Come, shepherd, and again begin the quest!   10

Here, where the reaper was at work of late—
  In this high field's dark corner, where he leaves
    His coat, his basket, and his earthen cruse,
    And in the sun all morning binds the sheaves,
  Then here, at noon, comes back his stores to use—
    Here will I sit and wait,
  While to my ear from uplands far away
    The bleating of the folded flocks is borne,
    With distant cries of reapers in the corn—
  All the live murmur of a summer's day.   20

Screen'd is this nook o'er the high, half-reap'd field,
  And here till sun-down, shepherd! will I be.
    Through the thick corn the scarlet poppies peep,

THE SCHOLAR GIPSY

And round green roots and yellowing stalks I see
   Pale pink convolvulus in tendrils creep ;
     And air-swept lindens yield
  Their scent, and rustle down their perfumed showers
     Of bloom on the bent grass where I am laid,
   And bower me from the August sun with shade ;
And the eye travels down to Oxford's towers.

And near me on the grass lies Glanvil's book—
   Come, let me read the oft-read tale again !
     The story of the Oxford scholar poor,   10
  Of pregnant parts and quick inventive brain,
     Who, tired of knocking at preferment's door,
       One summer-morn forsook
  His friends, and went to learn the gipsy-lore,
     And roam'd the world with that wild brotherhood,
   And came, as most men deem'd, to little good,
But came to Oxford and his friends no more.

But once, years after, in the country-lanes,
   Two scholars, whom at college erst he knew,
     Met him, and of his way of life enquired ;   20
  Whereat he answer'd, that the gipsy-crew,
     His mates, had arts to rule as they desired
       The workings of men's brains,
  And they can bind them to what thoughts they will.
     " And I," he said, " the secret of their art,
   When fully learn'd, will to the world impart ;
But it needs heaven-sent moments for this skill."

This said, he left them, and return'd no more.—
   But rumours hung about the country-side,
     That the lost Scholar long was seen to stray,   30
  Seen by rare glimpses, pensive and tongue-tied,

In hat of antique shape, and cloak of grey,
  The same the gipsies wore.
Shepherds had met him on the Hurst in spring ;
  At some lone alehouse in the Berkshire moors,
    On the warm ingle-bench, the smock-frock'd boors
Had found him seated at their entering,

But, 'mid their drink and clatter, he would fly.
  And I myself seem half to know thy looks,
    And put the shepherds, wanderer ! on thy trace ;
  And boys who in lone wheatfields scare the rooks
    I ask if thou hast pass'd their quiet place ; 11
    Or in my boat I lie
Moor'd to the cool bank in the summer-heats,
  'Mid wide grass meadows which the sunshine fills,
  And watch the warm, green-muffled Cumner hills,
And wonder if thou haunt'st their shy retreats.

For most, I know, thou lov'st retired ground !
  Thee at the ferry Oxford riders blithe,
    Returning home on summer-nights, have met
  Crossing the stripling Thames at Bab-lock-hithe,
    Trailing in the cool stream thy fingers wet, 21
      As the punt's rope chops round ;
  And leaning backward in a pensive dream,
    And fostering in thy lap a heap of flowers
    Pluck'd in shy fields and distant Wychwood
      bowers,
  And thine eyes resting on the moonlit stream.

And then they land, and thou art seen no more !—
  Maidens, who from the distant hamlets come
    To dance around the Fyfield elm in May,
  Oft through the darkening fields have seen thee
    roam, 30
    Or cross a stile into the public way.
    Oft thou hast given them store

THE SCHOLAR GIPSY

Of flowers—the frail-leaf'd, white anemony,
  Dark bluebells drench'd with dews of summer
     eves,
    And purple orchises with spotted leaves—
But none hath words she can report of thee.

And, above Godstow Bridge, when hay-time's here
  In June, and many a scythe in sunshine flames,
    Men who through those wide fields of breezy
     grass
  Where black-wing'd swallows haunt the glittering
     Thames,
    To bathe in the abandon'd lasher pass,
      Have often pass'd thee near   10
  Sitting upon the river bank o'ergrown ;
    Mark'd thine outlandish garb, thy figure spare,
    Thy dark vague eyes, and soft abstracted air—
  But, when they came from bathing, thou wast
     gone !

At some lone homestead in the Cumner hills,
  Where at her open door the housewife darns,
    Thou hast been seen, or hanging on a gate
  To watch the threshers in the mossy barns.
    Children, who early range these slopes and late
      For cresses from the rills,   20
  Have known thee eying, all an April-day,
    The springing pastures and the feeding kine ;
    And mark'd thee, when the stars come out and
     shine,
  Through the long dewy grass move slow away.

In autumn, on the skirts of Bagley Wood—
  Where most the gipsies by the turf-edged way
    Pitch their smoked tents, and every bush you see
  With scarlet patches tagg'd and shreds of grey,

Above the forest-ground call'd Thessaly—
The blackbird, picking food,
Sees thee, nor stops his meal, nor fears at all ;
So often has he known thee past him stray,
Rapt, twirling in thy hand a wither'd spray,
And waiting for the spark from heaven to fall.

And once, in winter, on the causeway chill
  Where home through flooded fields foot-travellers go,
    Have I not pass'd thee on the wooden bridge,
Wrapt in thy cloak and battling with the snow, 10
  Thy face tow'rd Hinksey and its wintry ridge ?
    And thou hast climb'd the hill,
And gain'd the white brow of the Cumner range ;
  Turn'd once to watch, while thick the snowflakes fall,
  The line of festal light in Christ-Church hall—
Then sought thy straw in some sequester'd grange.

But what—I dream ! Two hundred years are flown
  Since first thy story ran through Oxford halls,
    And the grave Glanvil did the tale inscribe
That thou wert wander'd from the studious walls
    To learn strange arts, and join a gipsy-tribe ; 21
    And thou from earth art gone
Long since, and in some quiet churchyard laid—
  Some country-nook, where o'er thy unknown grave
  Tall grasses and white flowering nettles wave,
Under a dark, red-fruited yew-tree's shade.

—No, no, thou hast not felt the lapse of hours !
  For what wears out the life of mortal men ?
    'Tis that from change to change their being rolls ;
  'Tis that repeated shocks, again, again, 30

THE SCHOLAR GIPSY

    Exhaust the energy of strongest souls,
      And numb the elastic powers.
Till having used our nerves with bliss and teen,
    And tired upon a thousand schemes our wit,
    To the just-pausing Genius we remit
Our worn-out life, and are—what we have been.

Thou hast not lived, why should'st thou perish, so?
    Thou hadst *one* aim, *one* business, *one* desire;
      Else wert thou long since number'd with the dead!
      Else hadst thou spent, like other men, thy fire! 10
    The generations of thy peers are fled,
      And we ourselves shall go;
But thou possessest an immortal lot,
    And we imagine thee exempt from age
    And living as thou liv'st on Glanvil's page,
Because thou hadst—what we, alas! have not.

    For early didst thou leave the world, with powers
      Fresh, undiverted to the world without,
        Firm to their mark, not spent on other things;
      Free from the sick fatigue, the languid doubt, 20
        Which much to have tried, in much been baffled, brings.
        O life unlike to ours!
    Who fluctuate idly without term or scope,
      Of whom each strives, nor knows for what he strives,
      And each half lives a hundred different lives;
    Who wait like thee, but not, like thee, in hope.

Thou waitest for the spark from heaven! and we,
    Light half-believers of our casual creeds,
      Who never deeply felt, nor clearly will'd,
      Whose insight never has borne fruit in deeds, 30

POEMS OLD AND NEW

Whose vague resolves never have been fulfill'd;
For whom each year we see
Breeds new beginnings, disappointments new;
Who hesitate and falter life away,
And lose to-morrow the ground won to-day—
Ah! do not we, wanderer! await it too?

Yes, we await it!—but it still delays,
And then we suffer! and amongst us one,
Who most has suffer'd, takes dejectedly
His seat upon the intellectual throne;　　10
And all his store of sad experience he
Lays bare of wretched days;
Tells us his misery's birth and growth and signs,
And how the dying spark of hope was fed,
And how the breast was soothed, and how the head,
And all his hourly varied anodynes.

This for our wisest! and we others pine,
And wish the long unhappy dream would end,
And waive all claim to bliss, and try to bear;
With close-lipp'd patience for our only friend,　20
Sad patience, too near neighbour to despair—
But none has hope like thine!
Thou through the fields and through the woods dost stray,
Roaming the country-side, a truant boy,
Nursing thy project in unclouded joy,
And every doubt long blown by time away.

O born in days when wits were fresh and clear,
And life ran gaily as the sparkling Thames;
Before this strange disease of modern life,
With its sick hurry, its divided aims,　　30
Its heads o'ertax'd, its palsied hearts, was rife—
Fly hence, our contact fear!

THE SCHOLAR GIPSY

Still fly, plunge deeper in the bowering wood !
Averse, as Dido did with gesture stern
From her false friend's approach in Hades turn,
Wave us away, and keep thy solitude !

Still nursing the unconquerable hope,
  Still clutching the inviolable shade,
    With a free, onward impulse brushing through,
By night, the silver'd branches of the glade—
  Far on the forest-skirts, where none pursue,
    On some mild pastoral slope   10
Emerge, and resting on the moonlit pales
  Freshen thy flowers as in former years
    With dew, or listen with enchanted ears,
From the dark dingles, to the nightingales !

But fly our paths, our feverish contact fly !
  For strong the infection of our mental strife,
    Which, though it gives no bliss, yet spoils for rest ;
And we should win thee from thy own fair life,
  Like us distracted, and like us unblest.
    Soon, soon thy cheer would die,   20
Thy hopes grow timorous, and unfix'd thy powers,
  And thy clear aims be cross and shifting made ;
    And then thy glad perennial youth would fade,
Fade, and grow old at last, and die like ours.

Then fly our greetings, fly our speech and smiles !
  —As some grave Tyrian trader, from the sea,
    Descried at sunrise an emerging prow
Lifting the cool-hair'd creepers stealthily,
  The fringes of a southward-facing brow
    Among the Ægæan isles ;   30
And saw the merry Grecian coaster come,
  Freighted with amber grapes, and Chian wine,
    Green, bursting figs, and tunnies steep'd in brine—
And knew the intruders on his ancient home,

The young light-hearted masters of the waves—
  And snatch'd his rudder, and shook out more sail ;
  And day and night held on indignantly
O'er the blue Midland waters with the gale,
  Betwixt the Syrtes and soft Sicily,
    To where the Atlantic raves
Outside the western straits ; and unbent sails
  There, where down cloudy cliffs, through sheets of foam,
  Shy traffickers, the dark Iberians come ;
And on the beach undid his corded bales.   10
                MATTHEW ARNOLD

ITYLUS

SWALLOW, my sister, O sister swallow,
  How can thine heart be full of the spring ?
  A thousand summers are over and dead.
What hast thou found in the spring to follow ?
  What hast thou found in thine heart to sing ?
    What wilt thou do when the summer is shed ?

O swallow, sister, O fair swift swallow,
  Why wilt thou fly after spring to the south,
  The soft south whither thine heart is set ?
Shall not the grief of the old time follow ?   20
  Shall not the song thereof cleave to thy mouth ?
    Hast thou forgotten ere I forget ?

Sister, my sister, O fleet sweet swallow,
  Thy way is long to the sun and the south ;
  But I, fulfilled of my heart's desire,

ITYLUS

Shedding my song upon height, upon hollow,
　From tawny body and sweet small mouth
　　Feed the heart of the night with fire.

I the nightingale all spring through,
　O swallow, sister, O changing swallow,
　　All spring through till the spring be done,
Clothed with the light of the night on the dew,
　Sing, while the hours and the wild birds follow,
　　Take flight and follow and find the sun.

Sister, my sister, O soft light swallow,　　　　10
　Though all things feast in the spring's guest-chamber,
　　How hast thou heart to be glad thereof yet?
For where thou fliest I shall not follow,
　Till life forget and death remember,
　　Till thou remember and I forget.

Swallow, my sister, O singing swallow,
　I know not how thou hast heart to sing.
　　Hast thou the heart? is it all past over?
Thy lord the summer is good to follow,
　And fair the feet of thy lover the spring:　　20
　　But what wilt thou say to the spring thy lover?

O swallow, sister, O fleeting swallow,
　My heart in me is a molten ember
　　And over my head the waves have met.
But thou wouldst tarry or I would follow,
　Could I forget or thou remember,
　　Couldst thou remember and I forget.

O sweet stray sister, O shifting swallow,
　The heart's division divideth us.
　　Thy heart is light as a leaf of a tree;　　30

But mine goes forth among sea-gulfs hollow
　To the place of the slaying of Itylus,
　　The feast of Daulis, the Thracian sea.

O swallow, sister, O rapid swallow,
　I pray thee sing not a little space.
　　Are not the roofs and the lintels wet?
The woven web that was plain to follow,
　The small slain body, the flowerlike face,
　　Can I remember if thou forget?

O sister, sister, thy first-begotten!
　The hands that cling and the feet that follow,
　　The voice of the child's blood crying yet,
Who hath remembered me? who hath forgotten?
　Thou hast forgotten, O summer swallow,
　　But the world shall end when I forget.
A. C. SWINBURNE

PIED BEAUTY

GLORY be to God for dappled things—
　For skies of couple-colour as a brinded cow;
　　For rose-moles all in stipple upon trout that swim;
Fresh-firecoal chestnut-falls; finches' wings;
　Landscape plotted and pieced—fold, fallow, and plough;
　　And áll trádes, their gear and tackle and trim.

All things counter, original, spare, strange;
　Whatever is fickle, freckled (who knows how?)
　　With swift, slow; sweet, sour; adazzle, dim;
He fathers-forth whose beauty is past change:
　　　Praise Him.
GERARD MANLEY HOPKINS

DRAKE'S DRUM

ROMANCE

I WILL make you brooches and toys for your delight
Of bird-song at morning and star-shine at night.
I will make a palace fit for you and me
Of green days in forests and blue days at sea.

I will make my kitchen, and you shall keep your room,
Where white flows the river and bright blows the broom,
And you shall wash your linen and keep your body white
In rainfall at morning and dewfall at night.

And this shall be for music when no one else is near,
The fine song for singing, the rare song to hear !   10
That only I remember, that only you admire,
Of the broad road that stretches and the roadside fire.
      R. L. STEVENSON

DRAKE'S DRUM

DRAKE he's in his hammock an' a thousand mile away,
 (Capten, art tha sleepin' there below ?),
Slung atween the round shot in Nombre Dios Bay,
 An' dreamin' arl the time o' Plymouth Hoe.
Yarnder lumes the Island, yarnder lie the ships,
 Wi' sailor-lads a-dancin' heel-an'-toe,
An' the shore-lights flashin', an' the night-tide dashin',
 Hè sees et arl so plainly as he saw et long ago.   20

Drake he was a Devon man, an' rüled the Devon seas,
 (Capten, art tha sleepin' there below ?),
Rovin' tho' his death fell, he went wi' heart at ease,
 An' dreamin' arl the time o' Plymouth Hoe.

" Take my drum to England, hang et by the shore,
  Strike et when your powder's runnin' low ;
If the Dons sight Devon, I'll quit the port o' Heaven,
  An' drum them up the Channel as we drummed
     them long ago."

Drake he's in his hammock till the great Armadas
     come,
  (Capten, art tha sleepin' there below ?),
Slung atween the round shot, listenin' for the drum,
  An' dreamin' arl the time o' Plymouth Hoe.
Call him on the deep sea, call him up the Sound,
  Call him when ye sail to meet the foe ;   10
Where the old trade's plyin' an' the old flag flyin'
  They shall find him ware an' wakin', as they found
     him long ago !
                    SIR HENRY NEWBOLT

THE HAWK

THE hawk slipt out of the pine, and rose in the sunlit air:
Steady and still he poised ; his shadow slept on the
     grass :
And the bird's song sickened and sank : she cowered
     with furtive stare
Dumb, till the quivering dimness should flicker and
     shift and pass.

Suddenly down he dropped : she heard the hiss of
     his wing,
Fled with a scream of terror : oh, would she had
     dared to rest !
For the hawk at eve was full, and there was no bird
     to sing,
And over the heather drifted the down from a bleed-
     ing breast.   20
                    A. C. BENSON

THE LAKE ISLE OF INNISFREE

I WILL arise and go now, and go to Innisfree,
And a small cabin build there, of clay and wattles made;
Nine bean rows will I have there, a hive for the honey bee,
And live alone in the bee-loud glade.

And I shall have some peace there, for peace comes dropping slow,
Dropping from the veils of the morning to where the cricket sings;
There midnight's all a glimmer, and noon a purple glow,
And evening full of the linnet's wings.

I will arise and go now, for always night and day
I hear lake water lapping with low sounds by the shore;   10
While I stand on the roadway, or on the pavements gray,
I hear it in the deep heart's core.

W. B. YEATS

THE SCHOLARS

BALD heads forgetful of their sins,
Old, learned, respectable bald heads
Edit and annotate the lines
That young men, tossing on their beds,
Rhymed out in love's despair
To flatter beauty's ignorant ear.

They'll cough in the ink to the world's end ;
Wear out the carpet with their shoes
Earning respect ; have no strange friend ;
If they have sinned nobody knows.
Lord, what would they say
Should their Catullus walk that way ?
                                      W. B. YEATS

JACK

I

EVERY village has its Jack, but no village ever had
    quite so fine a Jack as ours :—
So picturesque,
Versatile,
Irresponsible,
Powerful,
Hedonistic,
And lovable a Jack as ours.

II

How Jack lived none know, for he rarely did any work.
True, he set night-lines for eels, and invariably
    caught one,
Often two,
Sometimes three ;
While very occasionally he had a day's harvesting or
    hay-making.
And yet he always found enough money for tobacco,
With a little over for beer, though he was no soaker.

III

Jack had a wife.
A soulless, savage woman she was, who disapproved
    volubly of his idle ways.
But the only result was to make him stay out longer,
(Like Rip Van Winkle).

JACK

IV

Jack had a big black beard, and a red shirt, which was made for another.
And no waistcoat.
His boots were somebody else's;
He wore the Doctor's coat,
And the Vicar's trousers.
Personally, I gave him a hat, but it was too small.

V

Everybody liked Jack.
The Vicar liked him, although he never went to church.
Indeed, he was a cheerful Pagan, with no temptation to break more than the Eighth Commandment, and no ambition as a sinner.
The Curate liked him, although he had no simpering daughters. 10
The Doctor liked him, although he was never ill.
I liked him too—chiefly because of his perpetual good temper, and his intimacy with Nature, and his capacity for colouring cutties.
The girls liked him, because he brought them the first wild roses and the sweetest honeysuckle;
Also, because he could flatter so outrageously.

VI

But the boys loved him.
They followed him in little bands:
Jack was their hero.
And no wonder, for he could hit a running rabbit with a stone.

And cut them long, straight fishing-poles and equi-
    lateral catty forks ;
And he always knew of a fresh nest.
Besides, he could make a thousand things with his
    old pocket-knife.

VII

How good he was at cricket too !
On the long summer evenings he would saunter to
    the green and watch the lads at play,
And by and by someone would offer him a few
    knocks.
Then the Doctor's coat would be carefully detached,
    and Jack would spit on his hands, and brandish
    the bat,
And away the ball would go, north and south and
    east and west,
And sometimes bang into the zenith.
For Jack had little science :   10
Upon each ball he made the same terrific and magni-
    ficent onslaught,
Whether half volley, or full pitch, or long hop, or leg
    break, or off break, or shooter, or yorker.
And when the stumps fell he would cheerfully set
    them up again, while his white teeth flashed in
    the recesses of his beard.

VIII

The only persons who were not conspicuously fond
    of Jack were his wife, and the schoolmaster,
    and the head-keeper.
The schoolmaster had an idea that if Jack were
    hanged there would be no more truants ;
His wife would attend the funeral without an extra-
    ordinary show of grief ;
And the head-keeper would mutter, " There's one
    poacher less."

JACK

IX

Jack was quite as much a part of the village as the church spire;
And if any of us lazied along by the river in the dusk of the evening—
Waving aside nebulae of gnats,
Turning head quickly at the splash of a jumping fish,
Peering where the water chuckled over a vanishing water-rat—
And saw not Jack's familiar form bending over his lines,
And smelt not his vile shag,
We should feel a loneliness, a vague impression that something was wrong.

X

For ten years Jack was always the same,
Never growing older,
Or richer,
Or tidier,
Never knowing that we had a certain pride in possessing him.
Then there came a tempter with tales of easily acquired wealth, and Jack went away in his company.

XI

He has never come back,
And now the village is like a man who has lost an eye.
In the gloaming, no slouching figure, with colossal idleness in every line, leans against my garden wall, with prophecies of the morrow's weather;
And those who reviled Jack most wonder now what it was they found fault with.
We feel our bereavement deeply.

The Vicar, I believe, would like to offer public prayer
    for the return of the wanderer.
And the Doctor, I know, is a little unhinged, and
    curing people out of pure absence of mind.
For my part, I have hope ; and the trousers I dis-
    carded last week will not be given away just yet
                                    E. V. LUCAS

THE CHANGELING

TOLL no bell for me, dear Father, dear Mother,
    Waste no sighs ;
There are my sisters, there is my little brother
    Who plays in the place called Paradise,
Your children all, your children for ever ;
    But I, so wild,
Your disgrace, with the queer brown face, was never,
    Never, I know, but half your child !   11

In the garden at play, all day, last summer,
    Far and away I heard
The sweet " tweet-tweet " of a strange new-comer,
    The dearest, clearest call of a bird.
It lived down there in the deep green hollow,
    My own old home, and the fairies say
The word of a bird is a thing to follow,
    So I was away a night and a day.

One evening, too, by the nursery fire,   20
    We snuggled close and sat round so still,
When suddenly as the wind blew higher,
    Something scratched on the window-sill,
A pinched brown face peered in—I shivered ;
    No one listened or seemed to see ;
The arms of it waved and the wings of it quivered,
    Whoo—I knew it had come for me !
    Some are as bad as bad can be !

THE CHANGELING

All night long they danced in the rain,
Round and round in a dripping chain,
Threw their caps at the window-pane,
   Tried to make me scream and shout
   And fling the bedclothes all about :
I meant to stay in bed that night,
And if only you had left a light
   They would never have got me out !

  Sometimes I wouldn't speak, you see,
   Or answer when you spoke to me,
Because in the long, still dusks of Spring
You can hear the whole world whispering ;
   The shy green grasses making love,
   The feathers grow on the dear grey dove,
   The tiny heart of the redstart beat,
   The patter of the squirrel's feet,
The pebbles pushing in the silver streams,
The rushes talking in their dreams,
   The swish-swish of the bat's black wings,
   The wild-wood bluebell's sweet ting-tings,
     Humming and hammering at your ear,
     Everything there is to hear
In the heart of hidden things.
  But not in the midst of the nursery riot.
  That's why I wanted to be quiet,
   Couldn't do my sums, or sing,
   Or settle down to anything.
  And when, for that, I was sent upstairs
  I *did* kneel down to say my prayers ;
But the King who sits on your high church steeple
Has nothing to do with us fairy people !

'Times I pleased you, dear Father, dear Mother,
  Learned all my lessons and liked to play,
And dearly I loved the little pale brother
  Whom some other bird must have called away.

Why did they bring me here to make me
  Not quite bad and not quite good,
Why, unless They're wicked, do They want, in spite,
    to take me
    Back to Their wet, wild wood?
Now, every night I shall see the windows shining,
  The gold lamp's glow, and the fire's red gleam,
While the best of us are twining twigs and the rest
    of us are whining
    In the hollow by the stream.
Black and chill are Their nights on the wold
  And They live so long and They feel no pain :   10
I shall grow up, but never grow old,
I shall always, always be very cold,
    I shall never come back again !
                      CHARLOTTE MEW

STUPIDITY STREET

I SAW with open eyes
Singing birds sweet
Sold in the shops
For the people to eat,
Sold in the shops of
Stupidity Street.

I saw in vision   20
The worm in the wheat,
And in the shops nothing
For people to eat ;
Nothing for sale in
Stupidity Street.
                    RALPH HODGSON

ROUNDABOUTS AND SWINGS

It was early last September nigh to Framlin'am-on-Sea,
An' 'twas Fair-day come to-morrow, an' the time was after tea,
An' I met a painted caravan a-down a dusty lane,
A Pharaoh with his waggons comin' jolt an' creak an' strain ;
A cheery cove an' sunburnt, bold o' eye and wrinkled up,
An' beside 'im on the splashboard sat a brindled tarrier pup,
An' a lurcher wise as Solomon an' lean as fiddle-strings
Was joggin' in the dust along 'is roundabouts and swings.

" Goo'-day," said 'e ; " Goo'-day," said I ; " an' 'ow d'you find things go,
An' what's the chance o' millions when you runs a travellin' show ? " 10
" I find," said 'e, " things very much as 'ow I've always found,
For mostly they goes up and down or else goes round and round."
Said 'e, " The job's the very spit o' what it always were,
It's bread and bacon mostly when the dog don't catch a 'are ;   .
But lookin' at it broad, an' while it ain't no merchant king's,
What's lost upon the roundabouts we pulls up on the swings ! "

"Goo' luck," said 'e; "Goo' luck," said I; "You've
   put it past a doubt;
An' keep that lurcher on the road, the gamekeepers
   is out."
'E thumped upon the footboard an' 'e lumbered on
   again
To meet a gold-dust sunset down the owl-light in the
   lane;
An' the moon she climbed the 'azels, while a night-
   jar seemed to spin
That Pharaoh's wisdom o'er again, 'is sooth of lose-
   and-win;
For "up an' down an' round," said 'e, "goes all
   appointed things,
An' losses on the roundabouts means profits on the
   swings!"
                    PATRICK R. CHALMERS

TIT FOR TAT

HAVE you been catching of fish, Tom Noddy?
   Have you snared a weeping hare?
Have you whistled, "No Nunny," and gunned a
   poor bunny,
   Or a blinded bird of the air?

Have you trod like a murderer through the green
   woods,
   Through the dewy deep dingles and glooms,
While every small creature screamed shrill to Dame
   Nature,
   "He comes—and he comes!"?

Wonder I very much do, Tom Noddy,
   If ever, when you are a-roam,
An Ogre from space will stoop a lean face,
   And lug you home:

I MET AT EVE

Lug you home over his fence, Tom Noddy,
    Of thorn-stocks nine yards high,
With your bent knees strung round his old iron gun
    And your head dan-dangling by:

And hang you up stiff on a hook, Tom Noddy,
    From a stone-cold pantry shelf,
Whence your eyes will glare in an empty stare,
    Till you are cooked yourself!
                      WALTER DE LA MARE

I MET AT EVE

I MET at eve the Prince of Sleep,
His was a still and lovely face,   10
He wandered through a valley steep,
    Lovely in a lonely place.

His garb was grey of lavender,
About his brows a poppy-wreath
Burned like dim coals, and everywhere
    The air was sweeter for his breath.

His twilight feet no sandals wore,
His eyes shone faint in their own flame,
Fair moths that gloomed his steps before
    Seemed letters of his lovely name.   20

His house is in the mountain ways,
A phantom house of misty walls,
Whose golden flocks at evening graze,
    And witch the moon with muffled calls.

Upswelling from his shadowy springs
Sweet waters shake a trembling sound,
There flit the hoot-owl's silent wings,
    There hath his web the silkworm wound.

Dark in his pools clear visions lurk,
And rosy, as with morning buds,
Along his dales of broom and birk
    Dreams haunt his solitary woods.

I met at eve the Prince of Sleep,
His was a still and lovely face,
He wandered through a valley steep,
    Lovely in a lonely place.
          WALTER DE LA MARE

THE DONKEY

When fishes flew and forests walked
    And figs grew upon thorn,
Some moment when the moon was blood
    Then surely I was born ;

With monstrous head and sickening cry
    And ears like errant wings,
The devil's walking parody
    On all four-footed things.

The tattered outlaw of the earth,
    Of ancient crooked will,
Starve, scourge, deride me : I am dumb,
    I keep my secret still.

Fools ! For I also had my hour ;
    One far fierce hour and sweet :
There was a shout about my ears,
    And palms before my feet.
          G. K. CHESTERTON

CARGOES

Quinquireme of Nineveh from distant Ophir
Rowing home to haven in sunny Palestine,
With a cargo of ivory,
And apes and peacocks,
Sandalwood, cedarwood, and sweet white wine.

Stately Spanish galleon coming from the Isthmus,
Dipping through the Tropics by the palm-green
    shores,
With a cargo of diamonds,
Emeralds, amethysts,
Topazes, and cinnamon, and gold moidores.   10

Dirty British coaster with a salt-caked smoke stack,
Butting through the Channel in the mad March days,
With a cargo of Tyne coal,
Road-rails, pig-lead,
Firewood, iron-ware, and cheap tin trays.
                                JOHN MASEFIELD

PROMETHEUS

All day beneath the bleak indifferent skies,
Broken and blind, a shivering bag of bones,
He trudges over icy paving-stones
And *Matches! Matches! Matches! Matches!* cries.

And now beneath the dismal dripping night   20
And shadowed by a deeper night he stands—
And yet he holds within his palsied hands
Quick fire enough to set his world alight.
                                WILFRID GIBSON

THE SHIP

There was no song nor shout of joy,
    Nor beam of moon or sun,
When she came back from the voyage
    Long ago begun;
But twilight on the waters
    Was quiet and grey,
And she glided steady, steady and pensive,
    Over the open bay.

Her sails were brown and ragged,
    And her crew hollow-eyed,
But their silent lips spoke content
    And their shoulders pride;
Though she had no captives on her deck,
    And in her hold
There were no heaps of corn or timber
    Or silks or gold.
                Sir J. C. Squire

THE OLD SHIPS

I have seen old ships sail like swans asleep
Beyond the village which men still call Tyre,
With leaden age o'ercargoed, dipping deep
For Famagusta and the hidden sun
That rings black Cyprus with a lake of fire;
And all those ships were certainly so old
Who knows how oft with squat and noisy gun,
Questing brown slaves or Syrian oranges,
The pirate Genoese
Hell-raked them till they rolled
Blood, water, fruit, and corpses up the hold.

EVERYONE SANG

But now through friendly seas they softly run,
Painted the mid-sea blue or shore-sea green,
Still patterned with the vine and grapes in gold.

But I have seen,
Pointing her shapely shadows from the dawn
And image tumbled on a rose-swept bay,
A drowsy ship of some yet older day;
And, wonder's breath indrawn,
Thought I—who knows—who knows—but in that same
(Fished up beyond Aeaea, patched up new   10
—Stern painted brighter blue—)
That talkative, bald-headed seaman came
(Twelve patient comrades sweating at the oar)
From Troy's doom-crimson shore,
And with great lies about his wooden horse
Set the crew laughing, and forgot his course.

It was so old a ship—who knows, who knows?
—And yet so beautiful, I watched in vain
To see the mast burst open with a rose,
And the whole deck put on its leaves again.   20
JAMES ELROY FLECKER

EVERYONE SANG

EVERYONE suddenly burst out singing;
And I was filled with such delight
As prisoned birds must find in freedom
Winging wildly across the white
Orchards and dark-green fields; on; on; and
   out of sight.

Everyone's voice was suddenly lifted,
And beauty came like the setting sun.
My heart was shaken with tears ; and horror
Drifted away. . . . O but everyone
Was a bird ; and the song was wordless ; the singing
    will never be done.
SIEGFRIED SASSOON

THE DEAD

THESE hearts were woven of human joys and cares,
    Washed marvellously with sorrow, swift to mirth.
The years had given them kindness. Dawn was theirs,
    And sunset, and the colours of the earth.
These had seen movement, and heard music ; known
    Slumber and waking ; loved ; gone proudly friended ;
Felt the quick stir of wonder ; sat alone ;
    Touched flowers and furs and cheeks. All this is ended.

There are waters blown by changing winds to laughter
And lit by the rich skies, all day. And after,
    Frost, with a gesture, stays the waves that dance
And wandering loveliness. He leaves a white
    Unbroken glory, a gathered radiance,
A width, a shining peace, under the night.
RUPERT BROOKE

THE PIKE

FROM shadows of rich oaks outpeer
The moss-green bastions of the weir,
Where the quick dipper forages
In elver-peopled crevices,

THE PIKE

And a small runlet trickling down the sluice
Gossamer music tires not to unloose.

    Else round the broad pool's hush
        Nothing stirs,
Unless sometime a straggling heifer crush
Through the thronged spinney whence the pheasant
        whirs ;
        Or martins in a flash
Come with wild mirth to dip their magical wings,
While in the shallow some doomed bulrush swings
At whose hid root the diver vole's teeth gnash.   10

And nigh this toppling reed, still as the dead
    The great pike lies, the murderous patriarch,
    Watching the waterpit sheer-shelving dark,
Where through the plash his lithe bright vassals
    thread.

    The rose-finned roach and bluish bream
    And staring ruffe steal up the stream
    Hard by their glutted tyrant, now
    Still as a sunken bough.

    He on the sandbank lies,
        Sunning himself long hours   20
    With stony gorgon eyes :
        Westward the hot sun lowers.

Sudden the grey pike changes, and quivering poises
    for slaughter ;
    Intense terror wakens around him, the shoals scud
        awry, but there chances
    A chub unsuspecting ; the prowling fins quicken,
        in fury he lances ;
And the miller that opens the hatch stands amazed at
    the whirl in the water.

                              EDMUND BLUNDEN

PORTRAIT OF A BOY

AFTER the whipping, he crawled into bed;
Accepting the harsh fact with no great weeping.
How funny uncle's hat had looked striped red!
He chuckled silently. The moon came, sweeping
A black frayed rug of tattered cloud before
In scorning; very pure and pale she seemed,
Flooding his bed with radiance. On the floor
Fat motes danced. He sobbed; closed his eyes and dreamed.

Warm sand flowed round him. Blurts of crimson light
Splashed the white grains like blood. Past the cave's mouth
Shone with a large fierce splendour, wildly bright,
The crooked constellations of the South;
Here the Cross swung; and there, confronting Mars,
The Centaur stormed aside a froth of stars.
Within, great casks like wattled aldermen
Sighed of enormous feasts, and cloth of gold
Glowed on the walls like hot desire. Again
Beside webbed purples from some galleon's hold,
A black chest bore the skull and bones in white
Above a scrawled " Gunpowder ! " By the flames,
Decked out in crimson, gemmed with syenite,
Hailing their fellows by outrageous names
The pirates sat and diced. Their eyes were moons.
" Doubloons ! " they said. The words crashed gold.
  " Doubloons ! "

STEPHEN VINCENT BENÉT

WIT AND HUMOUR

SIR HUDIBRAS AND HIS SQUIRE
(From *Hudibras*)

When civil dudgeon first grew high,
And men fell out they knew not why;
When hard words, jealousies, and fears
Set folks together by the ears ;
When Gospel trumpeter, surrounded
With long-ear'd rout, to battle sounded ;
And pulpit, drum ecclesiastic,
Was beat with fist instead of a stick ;
Then did Sir Knight abandon dwelling,
And out he rode a-colonelling.   10
   A wight he was, whose very sight would
Entitle him Mirror of Knighthood,
That never bow'd his stubborn knee
To anything but chivalry,
Nor put up blow but that which laid
Right worshipful on shoulder blade ;
Chief of domestic knights and errant,
Either for cartel or for warrant ;
Great on the bench, great in the saddle
That could as well bind o'er as swaddle ;   20
Mighty he was in both of these,
And styl'd of war, as well as peace :
(So some rats of amphibious nature,
Are either for the land or water).
But here our authors make a doubt
Whether he were more wise or stout :
Some hold the one and some the other,
But, howsoe'er they make a pother,
The difference was so small, his brain
Out-weigh'd his rage but half a grain ;   30
Which made some take him for a tool
That knaves do work with, call'd a Fool,

For't has been held by many, that
As Montaigne, playing with his cat,
Complains she thought him but an ass,
Much more she would Sir Hudibras :
(For that's the name our valiant knight
To all his challenges did write).
But they're mistaken very much ;
'Tis plain enough he was not such.
We grant, although he had much wit,
H' was very shy of using it,   10
As being loth to wear it out,
And therefore bore it not about ;
Unless on holy days or so,
As men their best apparel do.
  For rhetoric he could not ope
His mouth but out there flew a trope ;
And when he happen'd to break off
I' th' middle of his speech, or cough,
H' had hard words ready to show why,
And tell what rules he did it by ;   20
Else, when with greatest art he spoke,
You'd think he talk'd like other folk ;
For all a rhetorician's rules
Teach nothing but to name his tools.
  A SQUIRE he had whose name was Ralph,
That in th' adventure went his half,
Though writers for more stately tone,
Do call him Ralpho, 'tis all one ;
And, when we can with metre safe,
We'll call him so ; if not, plain Ralph ;   30
(For rhyme the rudder is of verses,
With which, like ships, they steer their courses) :
An equal stock of wit and valour
He had laid in, by birth a tailor.
                        SAMUEL BUTLER

THE CHARACTER OF SHAFTESBURY
(From *Absalom and Achitophel*)

Of these the false Achitophel was first,
A name to all succeeding ages curst:
For close designs and crooked counsels fit,
Sagacious, bold, and turbulent of wit,
Restless, unfixed in principles and place,
In power unpleased, impatient of disgrace:
A fiery soul, which working out its way,
Fretted the pigmy body to decay
And o'er-informed the tenement of clay.
A daring pilot in extremity,
Pleased with the danger, when the waves went high,
He sought the storms; but, for a calm unfit,
Would steer too nigh the sands to boast his wit.
Great wits are sure to madness near allied
And thin partitions do their bounds divide;
Else, why should he, with wealth and honour blest,
Refuse his age the needful hours of rest?
Punish a body which he could not please,
Bankrupt of life, yet prodigal of ease?
And all to leave what with his toil he won
To that unfeathered two-legged thing, a son.
       JOHN DRYDEN

EPITAPH ON CHARLES II

Here lies our sovereign Lord the King,
  Whose word no man relies on,
Who never said a foolish thing
  Nor never did a wise one.
       EARL OF ROCHESTER

POEMS OLD AND NEW

THE COMBAT
(From *The Rape of the Lock*)

[As Belinda is taking coffee during a party at Hampton Court, the Baron obtains from Clarissa a pair of scissors, with which he cuts off a lock of Belinda's hair. She makes a moving speech. At the instigation of Thalestris, a general struggle ensues.]

SHE said: the pitying audience melt in tears,
But fate and Jove had stopped the Baron's ears.
In vain Thalestris with reproach assails,
For who can move when fair Belinda fails?
" To arms, to arms ! " the fierce virago cries,
And swift as lightning to the combat flies.
All side in parties, and begin the attack ;
Fans clap, silks rustle, and tough whalebones crack ;
Heroes' and heroines' shouts confusedly rise,
And base and treble voices strike the skies.　　10
No common weapons in their hands are found,
Like gods they fight, nor dread a mortal wound.
　So when bold Homer makes the gods engage.
And heavenly breasts with human passions rage ;
'Gainst Pallas, Mars ;　Latona, Hermes arms ;
And all Olympus rings with loud alarms :
Jove's thunder roars, heaven trembles all around,
Blue Neptune storms, the bellowing deeps resound :
Earth shakes her nodding towers, the ground gives way,
And the pale ghosts start at the flash of day !　　20
　While through the press enraged Thalestris flies,
And scatters death around from both her eyes,
A beau and witling perished in the throng,
One died in metaphor, and one in song.
" O cruel nymph ! a living death I bear,"
Cried Dapperwit, and sunk beside his chair.
A mournful glance Sir Fopling upwards cast,
" Those eyes are made so killing "—was his last.

THE COMBAT

Thus on Maeander's flowery margin lies
The expiring swan, and as he sings he dies.
  When bold Sir Plume had drawn Clarissa down,
Chloe stepped in, and killed him with a frown ;
She smiled to see the doughty hero slain,
But, at her smile, the beau revived again.
  Now Jove suspends his golden scales in air,
Weighs the men's wits against the lady's hair ;
The doubtful beam long nods from side to side ;
At length the wits mount up, the hairs subside. 10
  See, fierce Belinda on the Baron flies,
With more than usual lightning in her eyes :
Nor feared the chief the unequal fight to try,
Who sought no more than on his foe to die.
But this bold lord with manly strength endued,
She with one finger and a thumb subdued :
Just where the breath of life his nostrils drew,
A charge of snuff the wily virgin threw ;
The gnomes direct, to every atom just,
The pungent grains of titillating dust. 20
Sudden, with starting tears each eye o'erflows,
And the high dome re-echoes to his nose.
" Now meet thy fate," incensed Belinda cried,
And drew a deadly bodkin from her side.
(The same, his ancient personage to deck,
Her great great grandsire wore about his neck,
In three seal-rings ; which after, melted down,
Formed a vast buckle for his widow's gown :
Her infant grandame's whistle next it grew,
The bells she jingled, and the whistle blew ; 30
Then in a bodkin graced her mother's hairs,
Which long she wore, and now Belinda wears.)
    " Boast not my fall " (he cried) " insulting
      foe !
Thou by some other shalt be laid as low,
Nor think, to die dejects my lofty mind :
All that I dread is leaving you behind !

Rather than so, ah let me still survive,
And burn in Cupid's flames—but burn alive."
  " Restore the lock ! " she cries ; and all around
" Restore the lock ! " the vaulted roofs rebound.
Not fierce Othello in so loud a strain
Roared for the handkerchief that caused his pain.
But see how oft ambitious aims are crossed,
And chiefs contend till all the prize is lost !
The lock, obtained with guilt, and kept with pain,
In every place is sought, but sought in vain :
With such a prize no mortal must be blest,
So heaven decrees ! with heaven who can contest ?
  But trust the Muse—she saw it upward rise,
Though marked by none but quick, poetic eyes :
(So Rome's great founder to the heavens withdrew,
To Proculus alone confessed in view)
A sudden star, it shot through liquid air,
And drew behind a radiant trail of hair.
ALEXANDER POPE

ON A CERTAIN LADY AT COURT

I know the thing that's most uncommon ;
  (Envy be silent and attend !)
I know a reasonable woman,
  Handsome and witty, yet a friend.

Nor warped by passion, awed by rumour,
  Not grave through pride, nor gay through folly,
An equal mixture of good humour,
  And sensible soft melancholy.

" Has she no faults then," (envy says,) Sir ?
  Yes, she has one, I must aver ;
When all the world conspires to praise her,
  The woman's deaf, and does not hear.
ALEXANDER POPE

ELEGY ON THE DEATH OF A MAD DOG

Good people all, of every sort,
   Give ear unto my song;
And if you find it wond'rous short,
   It cannot hold you long.

In Islington there was a man,
   Of whom the world might say,
That still a godly race he ran,
   Whene'er he went to pray.

A kind and gentle heart he had,
   To comfort friends and foes;
The naked every day he clad,
   When he put on his clothes.

And in that town a dog was found,
   As many dogs there be,
Both mongrel, puppy, whelp, and hound,
   And curs of low degree.

This dog and man at first were friends;
   But when a pique began,
The dog, to gain some private ends,
   Went mad and bit the man.

Around from all the neighbouring streets
   The wond'ring neighbours ran,
And swore the dog had lost his wits,
   To bite so good a man.

The wound it seem'd both sore and sad
   To every Christian eye;
And while they swore the dog was mad,
   They swore the man would die.

POEMS OLD AND NEW

But soon a wonder came to light,
　That show'd the rogues they lied :
The man recover'd of the bite,
　The dog it was that died.
　　　　　　　　OLIVER GOLDSMITH

FRED

(Quoted in The Four Georges *by* JUSTIN MCCARTHY)

HERE lies Fred,
Who was alive and is dead.
Had it been his father,
I had much rather ;
Had it been his brother,
Still better than another ;　　　　　　　10
Had it been his sister,
No one would have missed her ;
Had it been the whole generation,
Still better for the nation.
But since it is only Fred,
Who was alive and is dead,
There's no more to be said.
　　　　　　　　ANONYMOUS

THE COLUBRIAD

CLOSE by the threshold of a door nail'd fast
・Three kittens sat : each kitten look'd aghast.
I, passing swift and inattentive by,　　　　20
At the three kittens cast a careless eye ;
Not much concern'd to know what they did there,
Not deeming kittens worth a poet's care.

164

THE COLUBRIAD

But presently a loud and furious hiss
Caused me to stop, and to exclaim—what's this?
When, lo! upon the threshold met my view,
With head erect, and eyes of fiery hue,
A viper, long as Count de Grasse's queue.
Forth from his head his forked tongue he throws,
Darting it full against a kitten's nose;
Who having never seen in field or house
The like, sat still and silent, as a mouse:
Only, projecting with attention due
Her whisker'd face, she ask'd him—who are you?
On to the hall went I, with pace not slow,
But swift as lightning, for a long Dutch hoe;
With which well arm'd I hasten'd to the spot
To find the viper. But I found him not,
And, turning up the leaves and shrubs around,
Found only, that he was not to be found.
But still the kittens, sitting as before,
Sat watching close the bottom of the door.
I hope—said I—the villain I would kill
Has slipt between the door and the door's sill;
And if I make despatch, and follow hard,
No doubt but I shall find him in the yard:—
For long ere now it should have been rehears'd
'Twas in the garden that I found him first.
E'en there I found him; there the full-grown cat
His head with velvet paw did gently pat,
As curious as the kittens erst had been
To learn what this phenomenon might mean.
Fill'd with heroic ardour at the sight,
And fearing every moment he would bite,
And rob our household of our only cat
That was of age to combat with a rat,
With out-stretch'd hoe I slew him at the door,
And taught him NEVER TO COME THERE NO MORE.
                                WILLIAM COWPER

POEMS OLD AND NEW

THE DESIRED SWAN-SONG

Swans sing before they die—'twere no bad thing
Should certain persons die before they sing.
                Samuel Taylor Coleridge

THE JACKDAW OF RHEIMS

The Jackdaw sat on the Cardinal's chair !
Bishop, and abbot, and prior were there ;
    Many a monk, and many a friar,
    Many a knight, and many a squire,
With a great many more of lesser degree,—
In sooth a goodly company ;
And they served the Lord Primate on bended knee.
    Never, I ween,
    Was a prouder seen,
Read of in books, or dreamt of in dreams,
Than the Cardinal Lord Archbishop of Rheims !

    In and out
    Through the motley rout,
That little Jackdaw kept hopping about ;
    Here and there
    Like a dog in a fair,
    Over comfits and cates,
    And dishes and plates,
Cowl and cope, and rochet and pall,
Mitre and crosier ! he hopp'd upon all !
    With saucy air,
    He perch'd on the chair
Where, in state, the great Lord Cardinal sat
In the great Lord Cardinal's great red hat ;
    And he peer'd in the face
    Of his Lordship's Grace,

THE JACKDAW OF RHEIMS

With a satisfied look, as if he would say,
" We two are the greatest folks here to-day ! "
  And the priests, with awe,
  As such freaks they saw,
Said, " The Devil must be in that little Jackdaw ! "

The feast was over, the board was clear'd,
The flawns and the custards had all disappear'd,
And six little Singing-boys,—dear little souls !
In nice clean faces, and nice white stoles,
  Came, in order due,   10
  Two by two,
Marching that grand refectory through !
A nice little boy held a golden ewer,
Emboss'd and fill'd with water, as pure
As any that flows between Rheims and Namur,
Which a nice little boy stood ready to catch
In a fine golden hand-basin made to match.
Two nice little boys, rather more grown,
Carried lavender-water, and eau de Cologne ;
And a nice little boy had a nice cake of soap, 20
Worthy of washing the hands of the Pope.
  One little boy more
  A napkin bore,
Of the best white diaper, fringed with pink,
And a Cardinal's Hat mark'd in " permanent ink."

The great Lord Cardinal turns at the sight
Of these nice little boys dress'd all in white :
  From his finger he draws
  His costly turquoise ;
And, not thinking at all about little Jackdaws, 30
  Deposits it straight
  By the side of his plate,
While the nice little boys on his Eminence wait ;
Till, when nobody's dreaming of any such thing,
That little Jackdaw hops off with the ring !

There's a cry and a shout,
And a deuce of a rout,
And nobody seems to know what they're about,
But the Monks have their pockets all turn'd inside out.
　　The Friars are kneeling,
　　And hunting, and feeling
The carpet, the floor, and the walls, and the ceiling.
　　The Cardinal drew
　　Off each plum-colour'd shoe,
And left his red stockings exposed to the view ;　10
　　He peeps, and he feels
　　In the toes and the heels ;
They turn up the dishes,—they turn up the plates,—
They take up the poker and poke out the grates,
　　—They turn up the rugs,
　　They examine the mugs :—
　　But, no !—no such thing ;—
　　They can't find THE RING !
And the Abbot declared that," when nobody twigged it,
Some rascal or other had popp'd in, and prigg'd it ! "
The Cardinal rose with a dignified look,　21
He call'd for his candle, his bell, and his book !
　In holy anger, and pious grief,
　He solemnly cursed that rascally thief !
He cursed him at board, he cursed him in bed ;
From the sole of his foot to the crown of his head ;
He cursed him in sleeping, that every night
He should dream of the devil, and wake in a fright ;
He cursed him in eating, he cursed him in drinking,
He cursed him in coughing, in sneezing, in winking;
He cursed him in sitting, in standing, in lying ;　31
He cursed him in walking, in riding, in flying,
He cursed him in living, he cursed him in dying !—
Never was heard such a terrible curse ! !
　　But what gave rise
　　To no little surprise,
Nobody seem'd one penny the worse !

THE JACKDAW OF RHEIMS

   The day was gone,
   The night came on,
The Monks and the Friars they search'd till dawn;
   When the Sacristan saw,
   On crumpled claw,
Come limping a poor little lame Jackdaw!
   No longer gay,
   As on yesterday;
His feathers all seem'd to be turn'd the wrong way;—
His pinions droop'd—he could hardly stand,—
His head was as bald as the palm of your hand;
   His eye so dim,
   So wasted each limb,
That, heedless of grammar, they all cried, "THAT'S HIM!—
That's the scamp that has done this scandalous thing!
That's the thief that has got my Lord Cardinal's Ring!"

   The poor little Jackdaw,
   When the Monks he saw,
Feebly gave vent to the ghost of a caw;
And turn'd his bald head, as much as to say
" Pray, be so good as to walk this way!"
   Slower and slower
   He limp'd on before,
Till they came to the back of the belfry door,
   Where the first thing they saw,
   Midst the sticks and the straw,
Was the RING in the nest of that little Jackdaw!

Then the great Lord Cardinal call'd for his book,
And off that terrible curse he took;
   The mute expression
   Served in lieu of confession,

And, being thus coupled with full restitution,
The Jackdaw got plenary absolution !
    —When those words were heard,
    That poor little bird
Was so changed in a moment, 'twas really absurd.
    He grew sleek, and fat ;
    In addition to that,
A fresh crop of feathers came thick as a mat !
    His tail waggled more
    Even than before ;
But no longer it wagg'd with an impudent air,
No longer he perch'd on the Cardinal's chair.
    He hopp'd now about
    With a gait devout ;
At Matins, at Vespers, he never was out ;
And, so far from any more pilfering deeds,
He always seem'd telling the Confessor's beads.
If any one lied,—or if any one swore,—
Or slumber'd in pray'r-time and happen'd to snore,
    That good Jackdaw
    Would give a great " Caw ! "
As much as to say, " Don't do so any more ! "
While many remark'd, as his manners they saw,
That they " never had known such a pious Jackdaw ! "
    He long lived the pride
    Of that country-side,
And at last in the odour of sanctity died ;
    When, as words were too faint
    His merits to paint,
The Conclave determined to make him a Saint ;
And on newly made Saints and Popes, as you know,
It's the custom, at Rome, new names to bestow,
So they canonized him by the name of Jim Crow !
                        R. H. BARHAM

KING CANUTE

King Canute was weary-hearted; he had reigned
    for years a score,
Battling, struggling, pushing, fighting, killing much
    and robbing more;
And he thought upon his actions, walking by the
    wild sea-shore.

'Twixt the chancellor and bishop walked the king
    with steps sedate,
Chamberlains and grooms came after, silversticks
    and goldsticks great,
Chaplains, aides-de-camp, and pages—all the officers
    of state,

Sliding after like his shadow, pausing when he chose
    to pause;
If a frown his face contracted, straight the courtiers
    dropped their jaws;
If to laugh the king was minded, out they burst in
    loud hee-haws.

But that day a something vexed him, that was clear
    to old and young: 10
Thrice his grace had yawned at table, when his
    favourite gleemen sung,
Once the queen would have consoled him, but he
    bade her hold her tongue.

"Something ails my gracious master," cried the
    keeper of the seal.
"Sure, my lord, it is the lampreys served at dinner,
    or the veal?"
"Pshaw!" exclaimed the angry monarch. "Keeper,
    'tis not that I feel."

" 'Tis the *heart*, and not the dinner, fool, that doth my rest impair :
Can a king be great as I am, prithee, and yet know no care ?
Oh, I'm sick, and tired, and weary."—Some one cried, " The king's arm-chair ! "

Then towards the lackeys turning, quick my lord the keeper nodded,
Straight the king's great chair was brought him, by two footmen able-bodied ;
Languidly he sank into it : it was comfortably wadded.

" Leading on my fierce companions," cried he, " over storm and brine,
I have fought and I have conquered ! Where was glory like to mine ? "
Loudly all the courtiers echoed : " Where is glory like to thine ? "

" What avail me all my kingdoms ? Weary am I now and old ;   10
Those fair sons I have begotten, long to see me dead and cold ;
Would I were, and quiet buried, underneath the silent mould ! "

" Nay, I feel," replied King Canute, " that my end is drawing near."
" Don't say so," exclaimed the courtiers (striving each to squeeze a tear).
" Sure your grace is strong and lusty, and may live this fifty year."

KING CANUTE

" Live these fifty years ! " the bishop roared, with
  actions made to suit.
" Are you mad, my good lord keeper, thus to speak
  of King Canute !
Men have lived a *thousand* years, and sure his majesty
  will do't.

 . . . . . .

" Did not once the Jewish captain stay the sun upon
  the hill,
And, the while he slew the foemen, bid the silver
  moon stand still ?
So, no doubt, could gracious Canute, if it were his
  sacred will."

" Might I stay the sun above us, good Sir Bishop ? "
  Canute cried ;
" Could I bid the silver moon to pause upon her
  heavenly ride ?
If the moon obeys my orders, sure I can command
  the tide."

" Will the advancing waves obey me, bishop, if I
  make the sign ? "   10
Said the bishop, bowing lowly, " Land and sea, my
  lord are thine."
Canute turned towards the ocean—" Back ! " he
  said, " thou foaming brine ! "

 . . . . . .

But the sullen ocean answered with a louder, deeper
  roar,
And the rapid waves drew nearer, falling sounding on
  the shore ;
Back the keeper and the bishop, back the king and
  courtiers bore.

And he sternly bade them never more to kneel to
   human clay,
But alone to praise and worship That which earth and
   seas obey :
And his golden crown of empire never wore he from
   that day.
W. M. THACKERAY

YOU ARE OLD, FATHER WILLIAM

"You are old, Father William," the young man
   said,
   "And your hair has become very white ;
And yet you incessantly stand on your head—
   Do you think, at your age, it is right ? "

"In my youth," Father William replied to his son,
   "I feared it might injure the brain ;
But now that I'm perfectly sure I have none,
   Why, I do it again and again."

"You are old," said the youth, "as I mentioned
   before,
   And have grown most uncommonly fat ;
Yet you turned a back-somersault in at the door—
   Pray, what is the reason of that ? "

"In my youth," said the sage, as he shook his grey
   locks,
   "I kept all my limbs very supple
By the use of this ointment—one shilling the box—
   Allow me to sell you a couple ? "

"You are old," said the youth, "and your jaws are
   too weak
   For anything tougher than suet ;

WASTE

Yet you finished the goose, with the bones and the
    beak—
Pray, how did you manage to do it?"

"In my youth," said his father, "I took to the
    law,
And argued each case with my wife;
And the muscular strength, which it gave to my
    jaw,
Has lasted the rest of my life."

"You are old," said the youth, "one would hardly
    suppose
That your eye was as steady as ever;
Yet you balance an eel on the end of your
    nose—
What made you so awfully clever?"   10

"I have answered three questions, and that is
    enough,"
Said his father; "don't give yourself airs!
Do you think I can listen all day to such stuff?
Be off, or I'll kick you downstairs!"
                                   LEWIS CARROLL

WASTE

I HAD written to Aunt Maud,
Who was on a trip abroad,
    When I heard she'd died of cramp
    Just too late to save the stamp.
                      HARRY GRAHAM

STAR TALK

"Are you awake, Gemelli,
    This frosty night?"
"We'll be awake till reveillé,
Which is Sunrise," say the Gemelli,
"It's no good trying to go to sleep:
If there's wine to be got we'll drink it deep,
    But rest is hopeless to-night,
    But rest is hopeless to-night."

"Are you cold too, poor Pleiads,
    This frosty night?"
"Yes, and so are the Hyads:
See us cuddle and hug," say the Pleiads,
"All six in a ring: it keeps us warm:
We huddle together like birds in a storm:
    It's bitter weather to-night,
    It's bitter weather to-night."

"What do you hunt, Orion,
    This starry night?"
"The Ram, the Bull and the Lion,
And the Great Bear," says Orion,
"With my starry quiver and beautiful belt
I am trying to find a good thick pelt
    To warm my shoulders to-night,
    To warm my shoulders to-night."

"Did you hear that, Great She-bear,
    This frosty night?"
"Yes, he's talking of stripping *me* bare
Of my own big fur," says the She-bear.
"I'm afraid of the man and his terrible arrow:
The thought of it chills my bones to the marrow,
    And the frost so cruel to-night!
    And the frost so cruel to-night!"

STAR TALK

"How is your trade, Aquarius,
 This frosty night?"
"Complaints are many and various
And my feet are cold," says Aquarius,
"There's Venus objects to Dolphin-scales, 5
And Mars to Crab-spawn found in my pails,
 And the pump has frozen to-night,
 And the pump has frozen to-night."
ROBERT GRAVES

NOTES TO THE POEMS

Sir Patrick Spens.
   The poet has confused the two following incidents :—
      1. In 1281, in the reign of Alexander III, a number of Scottish nobles accompanied Alexander's daughter Margaret to Norway, where she was to be married to King Eric. On the return voyage, a storm came on, and many of the nobles were drowned.
      2. On the death of Alexander III, an expedition was sent to Norway to bring over Margaret, the Maid of Norway, Alexander's granddaughter, heiress to the Scottish throne. On the voyage to Scotland, she died at Orkney in 1290.

P. 3, l. 1. *Dunfermline:* then capital of Scotland.
   l. 3. *Skeely:* skilful.
   l. 9. *Braid:* broad, *i.e.* important, probably a letter-patent, or open letter, with the royal seal.
   l. 19. *Neist:* next.
P. 4, l. 9. *Hoysed:* hoisted.
   l. 17. *Yestreen:* yesterday evening.
   l. 19. *Gang:* go.
   l. 23. *Lift:* sky.
   l. 24. *Gurly:* dark, stormy.
   l. 25. *Lap:* leapt, sprang.
P. 5, l. 3. *Wap:* to *knock* or stuff the material into the ship's side, by way of caulking the seams.
   l. 12. *Aboon:* above.
   l. 25. *Aberdour:* a port on the north shore of the Firth of Forth, about 5 miles from Dunfermline.

Helen of Kirconnell.
   Sir Walter Scott gives the following account of the occurrence on which this poem is founded :—
      " A lady of the name of Helen Irving, or Bell (for this is disputed by the two clans), daughter of the laird of Kirkconnell, in Dumfriesshire, and celebrated for her beauty, was beloved by two gentlemen in the neighbourhood. The name of the favoured suitor was

POEMS OLD AND NEW

Adam Fleming, of Kirkpatrick; that of the other has escaped tradition, although it has been alleged that he was a Bell of Blacket-house. The addresses of the latter were, however, favoured by the friends of the lady, and the lovers were therefore obliged to meet in secret, and by night, in the churchyard of Kirkconnell, a romantic spot surrounded by the river Kirtle. During one of these private interviews, the jealous and despised lover suddenly appeared on the opposite bank of the stream, and levelled his carbine at the breast of his rival. Helen threw herself before her lover, received in her bosom the bullet, and died in his arms. A desperate and mortal combat ensued between Fleming and the murderer, in which the latter was cut to pieces. The graves of the lovers are still shown in the churchyard at Kirkconnell."

P. 6, l. 7. *Burd :* maid.
l. 11. *Meikle :* much.

Rosabelle.

Sir Walter Scott (1771-1832). Born at Edinburgh and educated at the High School and Edinburgh University, Scott was trained to the law, and called to the Bar. From several years' residence in the Border district in his childhood, and from later visits, he amassed an enormous collection of ballad material, much of which he published in " The Minstrelsy of the Scottish Border " (1802). The interest thus fostered in feudal history found expression in a number of vigorous narrative poems, such as " The Lady of the Lake " and "Marmion." When Byron began to write the same type of poems, better, as Scott imagined, than himself, Scott turned to the novel, beginning with " Waverley " (1814), published anonymously. In 1826 Scott became involved in his publishers' bankruptcy, but, by his writing, had succeeded in clearing off a great part of the debt when he died at his country house at Abbotsford.

Scott is at his best in short poems, where his diffuseness is restrained by limit of form.

P. 7, l. 7. *Ravensheuch :* a large, strong castle, now ruined, situated between Kirkcaldy and Dysart, on a steep crag washed by the Firth of Forth.
l. 10. *Inch :* island.
l. 11. *Water-Sprite :* a spirit, whose screams were supposed to be an omen of disaster.

NOTES TO THE POEMS

l. 13. *Seer :* a man with second sight, or power to see into the future.

l. 18. *Roslin :* a castle, now in ruins, on the river North Esk, a few miles south of Edinburgh. It was founded about 1450 by Sir William St. Clair (Sinclair), baron of Roslin and Earl of Orkney.

l. 21. *The ring they ride :* to charge on horseback past a suspended ring and try to carry it off on the point of a lance.

l. 23. *Sire :* father.

P. 8, l. 3. *Dryden's groves :* an estate a mile north of Roslin.

l. 4. *Hawthornden :* the glen that runs north from Roslin Castle. Its steep sides, between which flows the Esk, are dotted with caves.

l. 5. *Chapel proud :* beside the ruins of Roslin Castle, stands the chapel. It contains a famous carved pillar. Cf. l. 11.

l. 8. *Panoply :* complete armour.

l. 10. *Sacristy :* the apartment where vestments, sacred books, etc., were kept.

Pale : rail, boundary.

l. 13. *Pinnet :* pinnacle.

l. 22. *With candle, book, and knell :* regularly—a common formula.

Proud Maisie.

P. 8, l. 25. *Maisie :* Mary.

P. 9, l. 3. *Braw :* handsome.

Bishop Hatto.

Robert Southey (1774-1843) belongs, with Wordsworth and Coleridge, to the group known as the "Lake Poets." He was a greater scholar than poet ; and so voluminous and detailed a writer that the very wealth of his information stifles his ideas. Hence only his slighter works now survive—his " Life of Nelson " (1813) and such short poems as " The Inchcape Rock " and " After Blenheim."

The story of this poem is a legend of an island in the Rhine, on which stands the Mouse Tower, and which is not far from Bingen.

La Belle Dame sans Merci.

John Keats (1795-1821) was born in London and apprenticed to a surgeon. He was a friend of Shelley and Leigh Hunt. His first long poem, " Endymion "

POEMS OLD AND NEW

(1818), illustrates the strength and weakness of Keats: it excels in rich sensuous descriptions and happy phrases but the story is lost (and remains unfinished) among the wealth of detail. The influence of Spenser is deeply marked. In his next volume, "Lamia, Isabella, and Other Poems" (1820), Keats illustrates the statement that he went to school with the great English poets. "Lamia" is in the style of Dryden, "Hyperion" is a Miltonic fragment, while many of the sonnets are Shakespearean in tone. These poems show a rapid development and his "Letters" prove that he was even more mature in mind than some of the poems might allow us to suspect. He was attaining to something of the literary perfection of his favourite Greece, when he died of consumption in Rome. Keats at his best is master of a Shakespearean felicity of phrase, and his early death robbed England of one of her potentially greatest poets.

P. 12, l. 22. *Zone*: girdle, belt.
  l. 23. *As*: as if.
P. 13, l. 2. *Manna dew*: cf. Exodus xvi. 15.

The Knight's Leap.

Charles Kingsley (1819–1875), Rector of Eversley, was keenly interested in social reform, and in his early novels, "Alton Locke" and "Yeast," he advocates a type of Christian socialism. His best novels, "Westward Ho!" and "Hereward the Wake," deal with historical adventure and the sea, in which as a Devonshire man he naturally delighted. His best poetic work is found in a few short lyrics like "The Sands of Dee"; while of his prose work "The Heroes," a group of Greek legends, and "The Water Babies" are still popular with the young.

P. 13, l. 27. *Ahr*: a western tributary of the Rhine, famous for the red wine produced in its valley.
P. 14, l. 1. *Harness*: armour.
  l. 7. *Trier*: Trèves, on the river Moselle, a tributary of the Rhine.
    Cöln: Cologne, on the Rhine, in Germany.

Horatius.

Thomas Babington Macaulay (1800–1859) was educated at Cambridge and, after being called to the Bar, entered Parliament and held several political posts.

NOTES TO THE POEMS

A retentive memory and enormous reading and information, together with a style rhetorical but of extreme lucidity and brilliance, qualified him to excel in historical writing. He first made his name at twenty-five with his Essay on Milton, published in the "Edinburgh Review." The "Lays of Ancient Rome" (1842) have the same qualities as his prose.

The Tarquin dynasty, expelled from Rome for the crime of Sextus Tarquinius, got support from the peoples of the surrounding districts, including Clusium, Tusculum, Veii, and Luna, and marched against Rome.

P. 15, l. 5. *Consul*: one of the two chief magistrates of Rome.

l. 12. *Lars Porsena*: King of Clusium.

P. 16, ll. 22-26. *Ramnian, Titian*: the Ramnes and the Tities were two of the three old patrician tribes of Rome. The third, the Luceres, was represented by Horatius.

P. 17, l. 9. *Fathers*: the Senate, the Roman parliament.

l. 13. *Tuscan (army)*: belonging to Etruria (Tuscany).

P. 18, l. 7. *Umbria*: the province north of Rome, and east of Etruria.

l. 19. *Luna*: a town in the extreme north of Etruria.

l. 29. *The she-wolf's litter*: the Romans. According to the legend, Romulus and Remus, the founders of Rome, were suckled by a she-wolf.

P. 19, l. 21. *Mount Alvernus*: a peak in the Apennines, in Etruria.

l. 25. *Augurs*: Roman officials who foretold future events from omens.

l. 33. *Lucumo*: a title of honour bestowed on Etruscan kings, nobles and priests.

P. 20, l. 7. *Etruria*: a province north of Rome, now Tuscany.

P. 22, l. 1. *Sextus*: the son of Tarquinius Superbus, King of Rome, through whose crime Tarquinius was deposed and banished from the city.

l. 9. *Palatinus*: one of the seven hills on which Rome was built.

l. 13. *Father Tiber*: Rome stands on the river Tiber.

P. 23, l. 32. *Volscian*: the Volsci lived in Latium, the province just to the south of Rome.

P. 24, l. 1. *Juno*: the queen of the gods, and wife of Jupiter.

POEMS OLD AND NEW

Shameful Death.
  William Morris (1834-1896), after an education at Marlborough and Oxford, began his career as an architect. His artistic temperament revolted from the monotonous drabness of an age of machinery, and he devoted himself to restoring something of the inspired craftsmanship of the Middle Ages. He joined the Pre-Raphaelite Brotherhood, founded for a similar purpose by D. G. Rossetti, Holman Hunt, and Millais, and included among his enterprises hand-printing, painting, poetry, and designs for wall-papers and house-decoration. In " The Life and Death of Jason " he approaches Chaucer in the ease and limpidity of his narrative, while in his lyrics he gives evidence of dramatic power.
P. 24, 1. 25. *Hornbeams :* a small tree commonly used for hedges.
P. 25, 1. 3. *Fen :* flat, marshy land.
  1. 4. *Dolorous :* mournful.

The Ballad of Semmerwater.
  Sir William Watson (b. 1858) came of a Yorkshire family. His numerous volumes of poetry, beginning with " The Prince's Quest " (1880), were written chiefly under the influence of Swinburne. His best work is done in the more simple ballad style.
P. 26, 1. 6. *Mickle :* great.
  1. 8. *Wakeman :* watchman.
  1. 20. *Brant :* steep.

Hart-Leap Well.
  William Wordsworth (1770-1850) was born and educated in the Lake District, where he spent a free and happy childhood. After a short period at Cambridge University, he travelled abroad, chiefly in France, just after the outbreak of the Revolution. His enthusiasm for France and the ideas of the Revolution suffered a severe shock with the September Massacres in 1792, and for the next few years he was in a state of deep depression and uncertainty. These years were spent at Nether Stowey, in Somerset, in the society of his sister Dorothy and his friend Coleridge. Through their influence and by his renewed contact with Nature, he gradually returned to his healthy youthful outlook, and in 1798 began the great period of his poetic production.

NOTES TO THE POEMS

In that year he issued "Lyrical Ballads," in collaboration with Coleridge. The book is a turning-point in literary history. Wordsworth discarded the artificial style of Pope and Johnson, and wrote of ordinary men and their primary emotions in the natural language of everyday life. Both emotions and language he found in their purest state in the country: hence his poems deal almost entirely with incidents and characters taken from country life.

P. 29, l. 1. *Wensley Moor:* in the Pennines round the head-waters of the River Ure.

l. 13. *Rout:* company.

P. 30, l. 15. *Yeaned:* weaned.

P. 31, ll. 19-20. *Swale, Ure:* tributaries of the Ouse, in Yorkshire.

P. 32, l. 13. *Hawes:* a town near the source of the River Ure.

Richmond: a town on the River Swale.

The Destruction of Sennacherib.

George Noel Gordon, Lord Byron (1788-1824), was born in London and educated at Harrow and Trinity College, Cambridge. He travelled much on the Continent, settling first in Switzerland, and afterwards in Italy. His travels are recorded in "Childe Harold's Pilgrimage." A rebel by personal and social circumstances, he favoured the French ideas of liberty and attacked fiercely the restrictions then imposed in England on social and political freedom. In 1823 he put his ideals into practice by fitting out a ship to help the Greeks in their war of liberation against the Turks. He was seized with fever and died at Missolonghi. His bravery in the cause of freedom, his resolute and romantic personality, as much as the force and romantic gloom of his poetry, made and have long kept him a European hero.

"Now in the fourteenth year of king Hezekiah did Sennacherib king of Assyria come up against all the fenced cities of Judah, and took them. . . . And the king of Assyria sent Tartan and Rabsaris and Rabshakeh from Lachish to king Hezekiah with a great host against Jerusalem. And. they went up and came to Jerusalem. . . . And it came to pass that night, that the angel of the Lord went out, and smote in the camp of the Assyrians an hundred fourscore and five thousand : and when they arose early in the morning, behold, they were all dead corpses. So Sennacherib king of Assyria departed, and went and returned, and dwelt at Nineveh."—2 Kings xviii. and xix.

P. 35, l. 5. *Assyria :* an ancient country in the valley of the river Tigris : now Iraq.
  l. 6. *Cohorts :* regiments, troops.
  l. 8. *Deep Galilee :* the Lake of Galilee, in Palestine.
P. 36, l. 1. *Ashur :* one of the chief towns of Assyria, and on the river Tigris.
  l. 2. *Baal :* a Phoenician god.
  l. 3. *Gentile :* any one who was not a Jew.

The Armada.

P. 36, l. 11. *Castile :* the more important half of Spain : here = Spain.
  Aurigny's Isle : a small island in the English Channel, just off Cape de la Hogue : Alderney.
  l. 16. *Edgecumbe :* a peak near Plymouth (facing Plymouth Hoe).
P. 37, l. 2. *Halberdiers :* soldiers armed with the halberd, —a long pole surmounted by an axe-head on one side and a hook on the other.
  l. 3. *Yeomen :* freeholders, a grade below gentlemen.
  l. 4. *Her Grace :* Queen Elizabeth.
  l. 7. *Lion :* the emblem of England.
  l. 8. *Gay lilies :* the emblem of France. On the English royal arms of that day the lilies of France still appeared in the quartering beneath the lion.
  l. 9. *That famed Picard field :* Crecy (1346), in Picardy, where Edward III defeated the French king, Philip VI.
  l. 10. *Bohemia's plume :* the King of Bohemia, fighting for France, was slain at Crecy. His triple feather crest, with the motto *Ich dien*, was adopted by the Black Prince, Edward's eldest son, who won his spurs in the battle.
  Genoa's bow : the Genoese archers on the French side at Crecy.
  Caesar's eagle shield : the imperial eagle of the House of Austria.
  l. 11. *Agincourt :* the battle in the North of France, where Henry V, in 1415, turned on the French and defeated them.
  l. 16. *Semper eadem : Lat.* always the same : the motto on the English royal standard.
P. 38, l. 2. *Eddystone :* a rock to the south of Plymouth.

NOTES TO THE POEMS

There is now a lighthouse on it.
  Lynn : in Norfolk, in the east of England.

  Milford Bay : in S.W. Wales, in the extreme west of Britain.

l. 5. *St. Michael's Mount*: in Mount's Bay, east of Land's End.
l. 8. *Tamar*: the river in Cornwall (Plymouth stands on its estuary).
l. 9. *Mendip's sunless caves:* the lead-mines, now exhausted, in the Mendip Hills.
l. 10. *Longleat's towers*: in Wiltshire.
  Cranbourne: an abbey in the north of Dorset.
l. 11. *Stonehenge*: the famous Druid circle on Salisbury Plain.
  Beaulieu: a town on the borders of the New Forest, Hampshire.
l. 13. *Clifton Down*: near Bristol.
l. 14. *Whitehall Gate*: in London.
l. 15. *Richmond Hill*: just south of London.
P. 39, l. 1. *The Tower*: *i.e.* of London.
l. 7. *Blackheath*: now in London, near Greenwich.
l. 10. *Hampstead*: Hampstead Heath, London.
l. 13. *Peak*: the mountain at the south end of the Pennine Chain.
  Darwin: in north Lancashire.
l. 15. *Malvern*: hills in Worcestershire just west of the Severn.
l. 16. *Wrekin*: a peak near Shrewsbury.
l. 17. *Ely's stately fane*: the cathedral of Ely, near Cambridge.
l. 19. *Belvoir*: (*pron*. Beevor) in Leicestershire, 7 miles S.W. of Grantham.
P. 40, l. 1. *Trent*: a tributary of the Humber.
l. 2. *Skiddaw*: one of the chief peaks in Cumberland.
  Gaunt's embattled pile: Lancaster castle, restored by John of Gaunt.
  Embattled: furnished with battlements.

Morte d'Arthur.

Alfred, Lord Tennyson (1809-1892) was the son of a clergyman and born at Somersby, in Lincolnshire. At Trinity College, Cambridge, he made the acquaintance of Arthur Henry Hallam, on whose death he wrote " In Memoriam." His early work, " Poems, chiefly Lyrical " (1830), shows him already a master of sound and rhythm, in the tradition of Spenser and Keats. In his later volumes, this power was increased and combined with a growing vein of serious thought on the social and religious questions of the day. " The Princess " (1847) dealt with the position and education

NOTES TO THE POEMS

of women, and " In Memoriam " (1850) with religious problems. Tennyson's poetry at its finest approaches the poetry of Virgil in perfection of language and emotional effect, and his acute powers of observation are reflected in the accuracy of his descriptions and character-studies. Tennyson is perhaps at his best in his lyrics, such as those in " The Princess," and in dramatic monologues, like " Ulysses," or poems like the ode " To Virgil " or " The Lotos-Eaters," where an atmosphere has to be created. His limitations—a straining, at times over-conscious, after effective expression, a vein of sentimentality, and a limited power of purely original thought—explain the decline which he has suffered from his first enthusiastic popularity.

In the *Morte d'Arthur* King Arthur had been mortally wounded in his last battle, and was now attended only by the last of his knights, Sir Bedivere. The following is Malory's account on which Tennyson's poem is based :—

" ' But my time hieth fast,' said King Arthur unto Sir Bedivere, ' therefore take thou Excalibur, my good sword, and go with it unto yonder water-side ; and when thou comest there, I charge thee, throw my sword into that water, and come again and tell me what thou shalt see there.' ' My lord,' said Sir Bedivere, ' your command shall be done, and lightly bring you word again.' And so Sir Bedivere departed, and by the way he beheld that noble sword, where the pommel and the haft were all of precious stones. And then he said to himself, ' If I throw this rich sword into the water, thereof shall never come good, but harm and loss.' And then Sir Bedivere hid Excalibur under a tree, and as soon as he might, he came again unto King Arthur, and said he had been at the water, and had thrown the sword into the water. ' What sawest thou there ? ' said the king. ' Sir,' said he, ' I saw nothing but waves and wind.' ' That is untruly said of thee,' said King Arthur, ' therefore go thou lightly and do my command, as thou art to me lief and dear, spare not but throw it in.' Then Sir Bedivere returned again, and took the sword in his hand ; and then he thought it sin and shame to throw away that noble sword ; and so after he hid the sword, and returned again, and told to the king that he had been at the water and done his command. ' What saw ye there ? ' said the King. ' Sir,' said he,

'I saw nothing but the waters wap and the waves wan.'
'Ah! traitor, untrue,' said King Arthur, 'now hast thou betrayed me two times, who would have weened that thou that hast been unto me so lief and dear, and thou art named a noble knight, and wouldest betray me for the rich sword. But now go again lightly, for thy long tarrying putteth me in great jeopardy of my life, for I have taken cold; and but if thou do as I command thee, and if ever I may see thee, I shall slay thee with mine own hands, for thou wouldst for my rich sword see me dead.' Then Sir Bedivere departed, and went to the sword, and lightly took it up and went to the water's side, and there he bound the girdle about the hilts. And then he threw the sword into the water as far as he might, and there came an arm and a hand above the water, and met it and caught it, and so shook it thrice and brandished. And then the hand vanished away with the sword in the water.

" So Sir Bedivere came again to the King, and told him what he had seen. 'Alas!' said the King, 'help me from hence; for I dread me I have tarried over long.' Then Sir Bedivere took King Arthur upon his back, and so went with him to the water's side; and, when they were at the water's side, even fast by the bank hovered a little barge, with many fair ladies in it: and among them all was a queen, and all they had black hoods; and they wept and shrieked when they saw King Arthur.

" ' Now put me into the barge,' said the King. And so he did softly, and there received him three queens with great mourning; and so these three queens sat them down, and in one of their laps King Arthur laid his head. And then that queen said, 'Ah! dear brother, why have ye tarried so long from me? Alas! this wound on your head hath taken overmuch cold.' And so then they rowed from the land; and Sir Bedivere beheld all those ladies go from him. Then Sir Bedivere cried, 'Ah! my lord Arthur, what shall become of me now ye go from me, and leave me here alone among mine enemies!' 'Comfort thyself,' said King Arthur, 'and do as well as thou mayest; for in me is no trust for to trust in: for I will into the vale of Avilion, for to heal me of my grievous wound; and, if thou never hear more of me, pray for my soul.'

NOTES TO THE POEMS

But evermore the queens and the ladies wept and shrieked, that it was pitiful for to hear them : and, as soon as Sir Bedivere had lost the sight of the barge, he wept and wailed, and so took the forest, and so he went all the night."

P. 40, l. 6. *Table*: the Round Table, at which sat King Arthur's knights.
    l. 7. *Lyonesse*: the land (now submerged) west of Camelot whence Arthur was supposed to have come.
    l. 24. *Camelot*: a legendary place in England where Arthur was said to have his palace and court.
    l. 26. *Merlin*: the wizard who guided Arthur's fortunes.
P. 41, l. 5. *Samite*: silk.
    l. 11. *Middle mere*: the middle of the lake.
    l. 12. *Lightly*: quickly.
    l. 34. *Dividing the swift mind*: hesitating.
P. 42, l. 10. *Betray'd thy . . . name*: Bedivere, *Lat.* verus, *true*.
    l. 12. *Feälty*: fidelity, loyalty.
    l. 17. *Lief*: dear.
P. 43, l. 10. *Conceit*: imagination, idea.
P. 44, l. 2. *The northern morn*: the Aurora Borealis.
P. 45, l. 35. *Casque*: helmet.
P. 46, l. 6. *Greaves*: armour for the legs (below the knee).
    Cuisses: armour for the thighs.
P. 47, l. 13. *Avilion*: Avalon, the legendary "island of the blest," the supposed abode near Glastonbury of King Arthur. Tennyson calls it Avilion ("the apple island").

The Lady of Shalott.

Shalott: a secluded island in which the action of the poem takes place.
P. 47, l. 31. *Camelot*: See Note on "Morte d'Arthur" above, P. 40, l. 24.
P. 48, l. 17. *Shallop*: a light open boat.
P. 50, l. 9. *Sir Lancelot*: the most famous of the Knights of the Round Table.
    l. 16. *The Golden Galaxy*: the Milky Way.

Hervé Riel.

Robert Browning (1812–1889) began his poetic career with "Pauline" (1833), written under the influence of Shelley. "Paracelsus" (1835) followed. His work gradually became more dramatic in intention, with "Strafford" and other dramas, "Dramatic Lyrics"

(1842), "Dramatic Romances and Lyrics" (1845) and "Men and Women" (1855). "The Ring and the Book," his longest poem (1868-1869), is perhaps his masterpiece. The main event of an otherwise uneventful life was his elopement in 1846, with Elizabeth Barrett, the poetess, to whom he was devotedly attached until her death, which took place in Florence. Most of his later themes are drawn from Italian sources. Browning's poetry excels in fertility of ideas, in grasp of psychological subtleties, in power of delineating queer abnormal characters, and in dramatic quality, but suffers from obscurity and irregularity of syntax, and lack of poetic—though never of mental—quality.

P. 53, l. 10. *The Hogue:* Cape de la Hogue, in Normandy.
   l. 14. *St. Malo:* a seaport in Brittany.
     Rance: the river that flows into the Bay of St. Malo.
P. 54, l. 3. *Starboard, port:* the sides of a ship, right and left respectively.
P. 55, l. 4. *Breton:* of Brittany, in N.W. France.
   l. 5. *Croisickese:* a native of Le Croisic at the mouth of the Loire, where this poem was written.
   l. 7. *Malouins:* natives of St. Malo.
   l. 10. *Offing:* the part of the sea nearer the horizon than the coast.
     Grève: the beach to the N.W. of St. Malo is called La Grande Grève.
     Disembogues: enters the sea.
   l. 14. *Solidor:* the Tower and Port of Solidor are at St. Servan, on the Rance, a short distance south of St. Malo.
P. 57, l. 1. *Rampired:* fortified.
P. 58, l. 10. *Bore the bell:* won the first place, was victorious.
   l. 13. *Louvre:* a great palace in Paris, now used partly as a museum.

The Pied Piper of Hamelin.
   This poem was written for, and inscribed to, a little son of the actor, William Macready.
P. 58, l. 19. *Brunswick:* a state in the west of Germany.
P. 59, l. 23. *Obese:* fat.
P. 61, l. 15. *Tartary:* now Turkestan, in Asia.
     Cham (from Kam): sovereign, ruler.
   l. 17. *Nizam:* the ruler of an Indian state.
   l. 21. *Guilder:* a former Dutch (or German) coin, value about 1s. 8d.

NOTES TO THE POEMS

P. 62, l. 14. *Julius Caesar . . . commentary*: this took place at Alexandria.

l. 30. *Nuncheon*: literally, noon-draught: a light refreshment taken at or after noon; luncheon.

l. 32. *Puncheon*: a large cask (72–120 gallons).

P. 63, l. 13. *Claret, etc.*: four well-known varieties of wine.

l. 15. *Rhenish*: Rhine wine.

l. 34. *Caliph*: the chief ruler in a Mohammedan country.

P. 64, l. 2. *Stiver*: any small coin.

l. 5. *Brook*: endure.

P. 66, l. 7. *A text*: "It is easier for a camel to go through the eye of a needle than for a rich man to enter into the kingdom of God."—ST. MATT. xix. 24.

P. 67, l. 3. *Transylvania*: a province, formerly in Hungary, now in Rumania.

l. 9. *Trepan*: to trap, ensnare, decoy.

Goblin Market.

Christina G. Rossetti (1830–1894), sister of Dante Gabriel, was born in London. "Goblin Market" (1862) and "The Prince's Progress" (1866) have a grace and sweetness partly due to the writer's acquaintance with Italian, and a colour that calls to mind her association with the Pre-Raphaelite group of painters. Her later poetry is devoted to religious themes.

The formation of the narrative is as follows:—the goblins tempt women to eat their luscious but uncanny fruits; a first taste produces a rabid craving for a second taste; but the second taste is never accorded, and, in default of it, the woman pines away and dies. Laura having tasted the fruits once, and being at death's door through inability to get a second taste, her sister Lizzie determines to save her at all hazards; so she goes to the goblins, refuses to eat their fruits, and beguiles them into forcing the fruits upon her with so much insistency that her face is all smeared and steeped with the juices; she gets Laura to kiss and suck these juices off her face, and Laura, having thus obtained the otherwise impossible second taste, rapidly recovers.

From W. M. Rossetti's Notes to the "Poems."

P. 67, l. 21. *Quince*: a hard, acid, yellowish fruit used for flavouring.

P. 68, l. 8. *Bullace*: a small wild plum, allied to the damson.

POEMS OLD AND NEW

P. 69, l. 25. *Wombat:* an animal like a small bear.
    l. 26. *Ratel:* a nocturnal animal allied to the badger.
P. 72, l. 21. *Pellucid:* very clear.
P. 74, l. 29. *Succous:* succulent, juicy.
P. 75, l. 3. *Baulked:* disappointed, hindered.
P. 78, l. 24. *Demur:* to hesitate, object.
P. 81, l. 20. *Wormwood:* a bitter plant, bitterness.
P. 83, l. 17. *Antidote:* a counteracting medicine.

A Runnable Stag.
    John Davidson (1857–1909), born in Renfrewshire, was for some time a schoolmaster, and later a journalist in London. His volumes of poetry, " Fleet Street Eclogues " (1893, 1896), " Ballads and Songs " (1894), " New Ballads " (1897), " Last Ballads " (1899), and his series of " Testaments," not sufficiently known, display high and daring imaginative power. He was drowned at Penzance.

P. 83, l. 28. *Harboured:* tracked to its refuge.
    Coomb: deep valley.
    l. 29. *Feathered:* a hunting term for " put the hounds direct on the trail."
P. 84, l. 3. *Brow, bay and tray:* the first, second, and third antlers.
    l. 7. *Brocket:* a stag in his second year.
    l. 12. *Beamed and tined:* the two main horns are called the beams, and the branches from them are called tines.
    l. 14. *Tufted:* beat.
    l. 26. *Tufter:* beater. In stag-hunting, hounds trained to drive the stag out of cover.

Hawke.
    Sir Henry Newbolt (*b.* 1862), educated at Clifton College and Corpus Christi College, Oxford, was called to the Bar in 1887 and became editor of " The Monthly Review." His poetry, which deals almost entirely with war by land and sea, is full of energy and catching rhythms. No poet has better expressed the spiritual ideals of the English public school.
    In 1759, during the Seven Years' War with France, Admiral Hawke gained a decisive victory over the French fleet in Quiberon Bay. The action took place during a storm and on a very rocky and dangerous shore. This naval victory, the most important since the Armada, averted a threatened invasion of England.
P. 86, l. 21. *Twenty of the line:* *i.e.* battleships.

NOTES TO THE POEMS

l. 22. *Brest*: the most important French naval station on the Atlantic coast.

He fell among thieves.
P. 87, l. 17. *Sometime*: former.
P. 88, ll. 6–7. *Yassin river*: *Laspur hills*: in the Chitral district, in the extreme north-west of India, on the borders of Afghanistan. A native rising took place in the district in 1895.
l. 10. *Wistaria*: a climbing shrub (with lilac-coloured flowers).
l. 23. *College Eight*: the boat crew.
l. 24. *Dons*: fellows or tutors of the college, who dine on a daïs or slightly raised platform.

The Highwayman.
Alfred Noyes (b. 1880) was born at Wolverhampton and educated at Exeter College, Oxford. He has dealt poetically with great historical actions, as in " Drake " (1908) and " The Torchbearers " (1922-25-30). Such shorter poems as " The Highwayman " and " The Barrel-Organ " have achieved wide popularity.

The Passionate Shepherd to his Love.
Christopher Marlowe (1563-1593) was born at Canterbury and educated at Cambridge. While still at the University, he began to write for the London stage. He belonged to the group of University Wits, who derived a precarious living from literature. He was killed at the age of twenty-nine in a tavern brawl at Deptford. His most famous play, perhaps, is " Dr. Faustus." His contributions to the growth of the secular drama were his stately yet elastic blank verse and his conception of the tragic protagonist. He also wrote a narrative poem, " Hero and Leander," completed by Chapman, and a few exquisite lyrics.
P. 97, l. 8. *Madrigal*: a kind of part-song, unaccompanied, in the pastoral style.
l. 11. *Kirtle*: gown, petticoat.

Winter.
William Shakespeare (1564-1616). Little is known for certain about the facts of Shakespeare's life. He was born in Stratford-on-Avon, educated probably at the local grammar school, may have gone to London as early as 1584 to seek his fortune, and became actor and dramatist. About 1610, having made sufficient money out of the success of his plays, Shakespeare retired to Stratford and bought New Place, a solid country house.

Shakespeare is the greatest poet of the world, and in his works the human heart in every mood finds perfect expression.

This lyric is sung by Winter at the end of " Love's Labour's Lost."

P. 98, l. 13. *Keel*: to skim, clean.
l. 15. *Saw*: saying, sermon.
l. 18. *Crabs*: crab-apples.

Fidele.

This song is sung over the body of Imogen in "Cymbeline."

P. 99, l. 10. *Thunderstone*: thunderbolt.
l. 11. *Censure*: opinion, judgement.
l. 14. *Consign*: seal (the bond of death).

Character of a Happy Life.

Sir Henry Wotton (1568-1639), born near Maidstone, in Kent, and educated at Winchester and Oxford, entered the Middle Temple and later held various diplomatic appointments. He left little in the way of literature except a few graceful and polished lyrics.

P. 99, l. 18. *Silly*: simple.
l. 20. *Still*: always.
P. 100, l. 7. *Entertains*: whiles away.

To Celia.

Ben Jonson (1573-1637) was educated at Westminster, and was successively bricklayer's apprentice, soldier, actor, and dramatist. He was an erudite classical scholar, and bestowed great pains on his dramas, which are largely founded on classical models. His chief contribution to English drama was his development of the comedy of " Humours," characters in whom one peculiar quality is exaggerated to the extent of caricature, as in " Every Man in his Humour," " Volpone," and " The Alchemist." His lyrics are full of grace and sweetness.

P. 100, l. 19. *Jove*: Jupiter, the king of the gods.
Nectar: the drink of the gods.

Hymn to Diana.

This song is sung by Hesperus in " Cynthia's Revels " (1600).

P. 101, l. 5. *Hesperus*: the evening star.
l. 9. *Cynthia*: another name for Diana, the goddess of the moon.

NOTES TO THE POEMS

The Village Preacher and *The Village Schoolmaster.*

Oliver Goldsmith (1728-1774) was the son of an Irish clergyman—the kindly Mr. Primrose of " The Vicar of Wakefield." After desultory studies at Dublin, Edinburgh, and Leyden, he travelled on foot over France, Switzerland, and Italy, earning his living by his flute. On his return to London, he produced various types of work: essays, collected in " The Citizen of the World " ; a novel, " The Vicar of Wakefield " ; two plays, " The Good-natured Man " and " She Stoops to Conquer " ; and a few poems, including " The Traveller " and " The Deserted Village." His kindly humour and universal good-nature shines through all he wrote, and a natural and limpid style of exquisite charm has placed his work among the classics.

P. 101, l. 24. *Passing*: very (surpassingly).
P. 102, l. 5. *The vagrant train*: beggars.
  l. 7. *Long-remembered*: here meaning 'with a long memory; store of memories.'
P. 103, l. 30. *Cypher*: to count, do arithmetic.
  l. 32. *Gauge*: to measure (volume).

The Tiger.

William Blake (1757-1827) was born in London and became an engraver and printer. He issued and illustrated his own poems, of which the best known are " Songs of Innocence " (1787) and " Songs of Experience " (1794). At his best Blake combines a childlike simplicity with the vivid imagery and penetrating vision of a fervid mystic.

The Solitary Reaper.

This poem was suggested by the following sentence from Wilkinson's " Tour of Scotland " :—

" Passed a female who was reaping alone : she sung in Erse as she bended over her sickle ; the sweetest human voice I ever heard ; her strains were tenderly melancholy, and felt delicious, long after they were heard no more."

Upon Westminster Bridge.

This poem should be compared with the prose description of the same scene in Dorothy Wordsworth's " Journal " :
" We mounted the Dover coach at Charing Cross.

The city, St. Paul's, with the river and a multitude of little boats, made a most beautiful sight as we crossed Westminster Bridge. The houses were not overhung by their cloud of smoke, and they were spread out endlessly, yet the sun shone so brightly and with such a fierce light, that there was even something like the purity of one of Nature's own grand spectacles."

She dwelt among the untrodden ways.
P. 106, l. 24. *Dove:* there is a river Dove in Derbyshire and a Dove Crag in Westmoreland.

Soldier, rest!
This song and the next are taken from "The Lady of the Lake."
P. 108, l. 14. *Fallow:* land ploughed but unsown.
l. 15. *Bittern:* a wading bird of the heron family.
l. 24. *Reveillé:* a morning signal for soldiers to rise.

Coronach.
Coronach: dirge, lament.
P. 109, l. 17. *Correi:* (corrie), a steep-sided circular hollow on a hillside.
l. 18. *Cumber:* trouble.

Pibroch of Donuil Dhu.
"This is a very ancient pibroch belonging to Clan Macdonald, and supposed to refer to the expedition of Donald Balloch, who, in 1431, launched from the Isles with a considerable force, invaded Lochaber, and at Inverlochy defeated and put to flight the Earls of Mar and Caithness, though at the head of an army superior to his own."—SIR WALTER SCOTT.
P. 109, l. 25. *Pibroch:* war music on the bagpipe.
P. 110, l. 8. *Inverlochy:* near Fort William, in Inverness-shire.
l. 20. *Targes:* shields.

Kubla Khan.
Samuel Taylor Coleridge (1772–1834), son of the Vicar at Ottery St. Mary, Devonshire, was educated at Christ Hospital and Jesus College, Cambridge. At the outbreak of the French Revolution, he engaged, with his friend Southey, in an idealistic plan for a new settlement in America, but he was too unpractical ever to carry out the project. He made friends with Wordsworth, with whom he issued "Lyrical Ballads"

NOTES TO THE POEMS

in 1798, Coleridge treating supernatural subjects and Wordsworth themes from everyday life. He lived for some time near Wordsworth, at Keswick; and later he moved to London, where he lectured on Shakespeare. Towards the end of his life he became a victim to opium, which deadened his intellectual powers. He successfully overcame this habit, however, and spent the last years of his life contentedly at Highgate.

Coleridge gives the following account of the composition of this poem :—

"In the summer of the year 1797, the Author, then in ill-health, had retired to a lonely farm-house between Porlock and Linton, on the Exmoor confines of Somerset and Devonshire. In consequence of a slight indisposition, an anodyne had been prescribed, from the effects of which he fell asleep in his chair at the moment that he was reading the following sentence, or words of the same substance, in 'Purchas's Pilgrimage': 'Here the Khan Kubla commanded a palace to be built, and a stately garden thereunto. And thus ten miles of fertile ground were enclosed by a wall.' The Author continued for about three hours in a profound sleep, at least of the external senses, during which time he has the most vivid confidence, that he could not have composed less than from two to three hundred lines; if that indeed can be called composition in which all the images rose up before him as *things*, with a parallel production of the corresponding expressions, without any sensation or consciousness of effort. On awaking he appeared to himself to have a distinct recollection of the whole, and taking his pen, ink, and paper, instantly and eagerly wrote down the lines that are here preserved. At this moment he was unfortunately called out by a person on business from Porlock, and detained by him above an hour, and on his return to his room, found, to his no small surprise and mortification, that though he still retained some vague and dim recollection of the general purport of the vision, yet, with the exception of some eight or ten scattered lines and images, all the rest had passed away like the images on the surface of a stream into which a stone has been cast, but alas! without the after restoration of the latter!"

The following is the actual passage that Coleridge was reading when he fell asleep :—

POEMS OLD AND NEW

"In Xamdiu did Cublai Can build a stately Palace, encompassing sixteene miles of plaine ground with a wall, wherein are fertile Meddowes, pleasant Springs, delightfull Streames, and all sorts of beasts of chase and game, and in the middest thereof a sumptuous house of pleasure."

P. 111, l. 5. *Xanadu :* Shandu.

Kubla Khan (1216-1294) : founder of the Mongol dynasty in China. He built Pekin as his capital.

P. 112, l. 13. *Abora :* Abba Yared, a mountain in Abyssinia.

The Parrot.

Thomas Campbell (1777-1844) was born in Glasgow and educated there and in Edinburgh. After travelling on the Continent, he settled in London and took up literary work. His long poems, "The Pleasures of Hope," "Gertrude of Wyoming" and "Theodric," have lost their popularity, which his shorter poems, by their energy and occasional felicity of phrase and rhythm, have retained.

P. 112, l. 27. *The Spanish main :* the northern mainland of South America, especially that part bordering the Caribbean Sea.

l. 30. *Mullah :* the island of Mull.

To Night.

Percy Bysshe Shelley (1792-1822) was educated at Eton and Oxford. He early adopted the rationalist ideas of William Godwin, whose daughter he afterwards married. With her he settled in Italy near to his friend Byron. On the death of Keats he wrote the elegy "Adonais." Like Keats, he died prematurely, being drowned while sailing in the Gulf of Spezzia. Shelley and Keats are both buried in the Protestant Cemetery in Rome.

Matthew Arnold said of Shelley that his proper sphere was not poetry but music. Certainly the superb rhythm and cadence of his verse are in essence musical, but when, as in "The Cenci," he set himself to treat a concrete theme his work is as thoughtful as such lyrics as "The Skylark" and the "Ode to the West Wind" are musical. Shelley's early death deprived England of one of the finest, if not the finest, of her lyric poets.

The Human Seasons.

P. 115, l. 25. *Ruminate :* to chew the cud.

NOTES TO THE POEMS

P. 116, l. 5. *Misfeature:* distortion or ugliness — a word coined by Keats.

On first looking into Chapman's Homer.

P. 116, l. 14. *Chapman:* an Elizabethan dramatist and poet. His translation of Homer, in heptameters, captures something of the spirit and movement of the original.

l. 17. *Cortez:* the conqueror of Mexico (1519-1521). This allusion is a mistake: the Pacific was first seen by Vasco Balboa (1513).

To Autumn.

P. 117, l. 28. *Sallow:* a kind of willow.

P. 118, l. 1. *Bourn:* boundary, limit. Keats uses the word here to mean "region."

Autumn.

John Clare (1793-1864), the Northamptonshire peasant-poet, wrote his earlier poems in the intervals of hard manual labour in the fields, and his later work in lucid intervals in a mad-house, to which ill-health, over-work, and drink had brought him. His best poems describe with clear natural simplicity and detailed accuracy the life of the country as he knew it.

P. 118, l. 13. *Rig:* ridge.

l. 19. *Cote:* dovecote.

l. 24. *Lea:* field.

Blow, bugle, blow.

This song is taken from "The Princess."

P. 119, l. 15. *Scar:* crag.

Home Thoughts, from Abroad.

P. 120, l. 6. *Bole:* trunk of a tree.

l. 10. *Whitethroat:* a small warbler.

l. 19. *Dower:* dowry.

O Captain! My Captain!

Walt Whitman (1819-1892) was born at Huntingdon, Long Island. He began work in a printing office, and after a varied career, became editor of "The Brooklyn Eagle" in 1846. In 1855 appeared his great work, "Leaves of Grass." In the Civil War he acted as nurse in the Federal army, an experience reflected in "Drum Taps." He then retired to New Jersey. His outlook is optimistic without being weak or blind—

what William James called "healthy-minded." He tried free verse with varying success.

The Captain was President Lincoln, who held office during the American Civil War and was assassinated just when he had achieved victory.

The Scholar Gipsy.

Matthew Arnold (1822–1888), eldest son of Dr. Arnold, the famous Headmaster of Rugby, was educated at Winchester, Rugby, and Balliol College, Oxford. After serving four years as private secretary to Lord Lansdowne, he was appointed an Inspector of Schools. During the thirty-five years which he held this Inspectorate he was sent on various occasions by the Government to inquire into methods of Continental education, and his reports had considerable influence in England. One of Matthew Arnold's greatest qualities was his desire to regard the culture of the world as a whole, and in criticism to avoid insularity. He was equally accomplished as a critic—his "Essays in Criticism" earned him the title of the English Sainte-Beuve—and as a poet—his best poetry, classic in style and beauty, wears as well as that of any of the Victorian poets.

For ten years he was Professor of Poetry at Oxford. He is buried where he was born, at Laleham, near Staines.

P. 122, l. 2. *Wattled :* of wicker-work.
    Cotes : sheep-folds.
  l. 10. *The quest :* the search for truth or certainty.
  l. 13. *Cruse :* jar, jug.
P. 123, l. 5. *Bent grass :* a rush-like grass with a stiff stem.
  l. 8. *Glanvil :* an English churchman (1636–1680) who wrote various theological works developing the ideas of Descartes.
  l. 11. *Parts :* accomplishments, ability.
  l. 19. *Erst :* formerly.
P. 124, l. 3. *The Hurst :* a wooded hill S.W. of Oxford.
  l. 5. *Ingle :* fire-side.
  l. 25. *Wychwood :* Wychwood Forest, north of Witney, about 14 miles N.W. of Oxford.
P. 125, l. 9. *Lasher :* the pool below a weir.
P. 126, l. 6. *The spark :* i.e. of inspiration.
  l. 11. *Hinksey :* North and South Hinksey lie between Oxford and Cumnor (see *Map*).
P. 127, l. 3. *Teen :* trouble.
  l. 5. *The just-pausing Genius :* the attendant spirit sup-

NOTES TO THE POEMS

posed to preside over each man's life and destiny. It pauses, or delays, long enough to give him a chance to show his powers, before putting an end to his career.

l. 11. *Peers:* equals, companions.

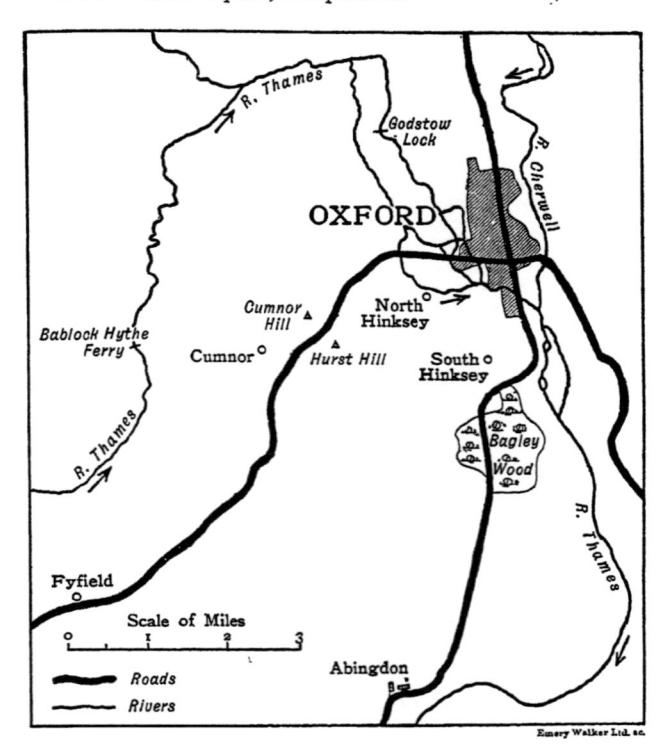

P. 128, ll. 8-9. *One, who most has suffer'd:* this can hardly apply to anyone but Goethe, the greatest of German writers (1749-1832), who in his youth wrote "The Sorrows of Werther," a novel chiefly autobiographical. Arnold considered him the greatest "modern man," and learnt from him many of his leading ideas, including that of Culture.

203

POEMS OLD AND NEW

l. 16. *Anodynes*: remedies to soothe or kill pain.
P. 129, l. 2. *Averse*: turning away.
   As Dido did: Dido, Queen of Carthage, who killed herself for love of her "false friend," Aeneas.
   Illa solo fixos oculos aversa tenebat. . . .
   Tandem corripuit sese, atque inimica refugit.
                    Virgil, "Aeneid," vi. 469, 472.
l. 26. *Tyrian*: of Tyre, on the coast of Palestine.
l. 30. *Ægæan Isles*: a number of small islands between Greece and Asia Minor.
l. 32. *Chian*: of Chios, one of the Aegean Islands.
l. 33. *Tunnies*: a large Mediterranean sea-fish.
P. 130, l. 5. *Syrtes*: two bays on the north coast of Africa, now known as the Gulf of Sydra and the Gulf of Gabes. Also: the sandbanks north of these bays.
l. 9. *Iberians*: the early inhabitants of Spain, the Iberian peninsula.

Itylus.
   Algernon Charles Swinburne (1837-1909) was born in London, and educated at Eton and Balliol College, Oxford. With "Atalanta in Calydon" (1865) he achieved poetic fame. His poetry shows a matchless command of rhythm and sound, and much of it was inspired by sympathy with the cause of political liberty abroad.
P. 130, l. 11. *Swallow, my sister*: According to the Greek legend, Pandius, king of Athens, had two daughters, Philomela and Procne. He called in against his enemies the assistance of Tereus, king of the Thracians in Daulis, and afterwards gave him his daughter Procne in marriage. Later, wishing to marry her sister Philomela, Tereus concealed Procne in the country and gave out that she was dead. At the same time he deprived Philomela of her tongue. Philomela, however, discovered the truth and made it known to her sister by a few words woven into a web. Procne thereupon killed her son Itys, and served up the flesh to Tereus. The sisters then fled, pursued by Tereus. When overtaken, they prayed to the gods to change them into birds. Procne became a swallow, Philomela a nightingale.
   Swinburne has confused Itys with Itylus.
P. 132, l. 2. *Itylus*: Aëdon, wife of Zethus, king of Thebes, had one child, Itylus. Being envious of the twelve

NOTES TO THE POEMS

children of her sister-in-law Niobe, she resolved to kill the eldest of them, but in mistake slew her own son. Zeus, to avert her husband's vengeance, turned her into a nightingale.

l. 3. *Daulis:* a town about ten miles north of the Gulf of Cornith, but not near the Thracian Sea.

Thracian Sea: the northern part of the Aegean Sea.

Pied Beauty.

Gerard Manley Hopkins (1844–1889) lived and wrote in the Victorian era, but his poems were not published until 1918. He combined a vivid sense of the beauty of the external world with a deep insight into the soul. The experiments in metre and language that have prevented his popularity, are yet the sign of a vital imaginative energy conspicuous among the Victorians.

In the Preface to his "Poems," Father Hopkins calls "Pied Beauty" a Curtal-Sonnet, that is a sonnet "constructed in proportions resembling those of the sonnet proper, namely $6+4$ instead of $8+6$, with, however, a half-line tailpiece (so that the equation is rather $\frac{12}{2} + \frac{9}{2} = \frac{21}{2} = 10\frac{1}{2}$)."

A Passer-By.

Robert Bridges (1844–1930) was educated at Eton and Corpus Christi College, Oxford, and studied medicine. In 1913 he was appointed Poet Laureate. His works include various plays, critical essays, and "The Testament of Beauty." His interest in the mechanics of his craft and verse experiment is evident in his study, "Milton's Prosody," and in the exquisite workmanship of his own poetry. On its appearance "The Testament of Beauty" was hailed as likely to become a classic in English poetry.

The Vagabond.

Robert Louis Stevenson (1850–1894) was born and educated in Edinburgh. In 1875 he was called to the Bar, but never practised. He was forced to travel for his health, and finally settled in Samoa. His fame rests chiefly on "Treasure Island," "Kidnapped," "The Black Arrow," and other tales of adventure, told in a style carefully polished to a French clearness and precision.

POEMS OLD AND NEW

Drake's Drum.

P. 135, l. 15. *Round shot :* used to sink the body of a sailor buried at sea.

Nombre Dios Bay : near Porto Bello (in Central America), on the Isthmus of Panama.

l. 16. *Plymouth Hoe :* the stretch of flat ground (now an esplanade) at the head of Plymouth Sound.

l. 17. *The Island :* Drake's Island, in Plymouth Sound.

P. 136, l. 3. *The Dons :* the Spaniards.

l. 11. *The old trade :* buccaneering.

l. 12. *Ware :* aware, watching.

The Hawk.

Arthur Christopher Benson (1862-1925), an Eton housemaster and later President of Magdalene College, Cambridge, is chiefly known by his essays and contemplative work. He wrote also studies of Pater and FitzGerald in the " English Men of Letters " series.

The Lake Isle of Innisfree.

William Butler Yeats (*b.* 1865), born in Dublin and educated at Godolphin School, Hammersmith, took to art, but left it for literature. He took a prominent part in the revival of Irish drama at the beginning of the century. His prose work includes " The Celtic Twilight " (1893) and " Ideas of Good and Evil " (1903). The beauty—and the weakness—of his poetry, lies in its magical and romantic atmosphere.

P. 137, l. 1. *Innisfree :* an island in Lough Gill, near Sligo.

l. 3. *nine :* the perfect number.

The Scholars.

P. 137, l. 15. *Annotate :* to write notes on.

P. 138, l. 6. *Catullus :* a Roman poet of the first century B.C., who lived a riotous life and wrote the finest Latin love-poetry.

Jack.

Edward Verrall Lucas (*b.* 1868) was born at Brighton and educated at University College, London. After much journalistic experience, he became chairman of Methuen's. The main trend of his versatile writings is toward fancy and humour. He writes well of travel,

NOTES TO THE POEMS

  art, and literature, has made numerous anthologies, and is an authority on Charles Lamb.
P. 138, l. 12. *Hedonistic :* pleasure-loving.
  l. 24. *Rip Van Winkle :* the hero of Washington Irving's story, who was henpecked, went hunting in the mountains, and slept there for twenty years.
P. 139, l. 12. *Cutties :* short clay tobacco pipes.
P. 140, l. 1. *Catty forks :* forked pieces of stick used to make catapults.
  l. 9. *Zenith :* the point of the heavens directly overhead.
  l. 12. *Half volley, etc. :* cricketing terms.
P. 141, l. 3. *Nebulae :* clouds, mists.
  l. 7. *Shag :* coarse tobacco.

The Changeling.
  Charlotte Mew (1870–1928) lived a life of hardship, poverty, and ill-health, and finally committed suicide. Her life is reflected in her two volumes of poetry, " The Farmer's Bride " (1916) and " The Rambling Sailor " (1929).
  Changeling : a child substituted, generally by fairies, for another child.
P. 143, l. 15. *Redstart :* a small singing bird, allied to the redbreast and the nightingale.
P. 144, l. 9. *Wold :* open country, downland.

Stupidity Street.
  Ralph Hodgson (b. 1871) is best known by poems expressing sympathy for animals, and indignation with those who ill-treat them. " The Bull " is one of his most notable longer poems.

Roundabouts and Swings.
  Patrick R. Chalmers (b. 1872) was educated at Rugby, and is the managing director of a private banking firm. He has written two volumes of verse, " Green Days and Blue Days " (1912) and " A Peck o' Maut " (1914), and has contributed frequently to " Punch."
P. 145, l. 4. *Pharaoh :* gipsy (*i.e.* Egyptian).
  l. 7. *Lurcher :* a dog, half collie, half greyhound.
P. 146, l. 5. *Night-jar :* the goatsucker.

Tit for Tat.
  Walter de la Mare (b. 1873) is best known by his " Peacock Pie " and similar poems for 'the young of all ages.'

His delicate fancy excels in the treatment of supernatural or fairy subjects which require the creation of an atmosphere of mystery or romance.

The Donkey.

Gilbert Keith Chesterton (*b.* 1874) was born in Kensington and studied at St. Paul's School and the Slade School of Art. He gives the impression of abounding energy and spontaneity, and there is usually sound sense beneath the glitter of his paradox. His work is mainly directed against the narrowness of Puritanism, and finds expression through such various channels as the Father Brown detective stories, historical works, novels, poems, and essays. He has written lively studies of his favourite authors, Dickens, Browning, and Chaucer.

P. 148, ll. 23-24. See St. Matt. xxi. 1-9.

Cargoes.

John Masefield (*b.* 1878) in his youth ran away to sea, where he acquired, under compulsion, the faculty of telling a good yarn, shown in "A Tarpaulin Muster." "The Everlasting Mercy" (1911) created a sensation by its realism and narrative power. It was followed by "The Widow in the Bye Street" (1912), "Dauber," "Reynard the Fox" (1919), and other volumes. Masefield has also written several novels—"Captain Margaret," "Sard Harker"—and dramas—"Nan," "Philip the King." The popularity of his work was recognised in his appointment as Poet Laureate, in 1930.

P. 149, l. 1. *Quinquireme :* a galley with five banks of oars.

Nineveh : the ancient capital of Assyria : on the Tigris.

Ophir : a region possibly in S. Arabia, whence the Jews obtained gold and precious stones.

ll. 3-5. See 1 Kings x.

l. 6. *Isthmus : i.e.* of Panama.

l. 10. *Moidore :* a Portuguese gold coin, now obsolete.

Prometheus.

Wilfrid Wilson Gibson (*b.* 1878) shows the romantic influence of Tennyson in his early volumes, "Urlyn the Harper" (1900) and "The Queen's Vigil" (1902). With "Daily Bread" (1910) his attitude became realistic, and his theme the lives of ordinary men and

NOTES TO THE POEMS

women. He has also written several plays, including "Between Fairs" (1928).
Prometheus: a Greek who stole fire from heaven for the use of men.
P. 149, l. 22. *Palsied:* paralysed, helpless.
l. 23. *Quick:* live, as in "quicksilver," "the quick and the dead."

The Ship.

Sir John Squire (*b.* 1884), educated at Blundell's School and St. John's College, Cambridge, is editor of the "London Mercury," and contributes literary criticism regularly to the "Sunday Times" and the "Daily Telegraph." He is also editor of the "English Men of Letters" series. Critic, essayist, poet, and athlete, chairman of the Architecture Club, and secretary of the Stonehenge Preservation Society, his interests are wide as they are vital, and his influence is always on the side of sanity in letters and art.

The Old Ships.

James Elroy Flecker (1884-1915) entered the Consular Service in 1910, and was appointed to Constantinople. His close acquaintance with the East produced the rich imagery of his play "Hassan" and "The Golden Journey to Samarkand" (1913). In 1913 his health obliged him to go to Switzerland. He died of consumption at Davos.
P. 151, l. 12. *That bald-headed seaman:* Ulysses, who, on his return from the siege of Troy to his native island of Ithaca, wandered for long in the Mediterranean. His adventures are described in the "Odyssey" of Homer.
l. 15. *Wooden horse:* A device of Ulysses. The Greek army pretended to abandon the siege; but left behind a wooden horse. The Trojans dragged it into the town. In the night, the Greeks returned, the gates were opened by men who had been concealed within the horse, and Troy was taken.

Everyone Sang.

Siegfried Loraine Sassoon (*b.* 1886) was educated at Marlborough and Cambridge. He served with distinction in France and later in Palestine. His revulsion from war found vent in his "Collected War Poems" (1919), "Satirical Poems" (1926), and "Memoirs of an Infantry Officer" (1930). His love of the

POEMS OLD AND NEW

English countryside runs through the "Memoirs of a Fox-Hunting Man" (1928).

The Dead.
Rupert Brooke (1887-1915), educated at Rugby and Cambridge, joined the R.N.V.R. at the outbreak of war in 1914, served at Antwerp, and died of blood poisoning from an insect bite at Skyros, on his way to the Dardanelles. His "Poems" (1911) and "1914 and Other Poems" (1915) express poignantly and vividly the joys, sorrows, and aspirations of youth.

The Pike.
Edmund Charles Blunden (*b.* 1896) was Professor of English Literature at Tokio University (1924-1927). His poems, informed by a love of the English countryside, include "The Waggoner" (1920), "The Shepherd" (1922), "To Nature" (1923), "Masks of Time" (1925), and "English Poems" (1928). He has also written a volume of war reminiscences, "Undertones of War."

P. 152, l. 21. *Bastion:* a kind of tower at the angles of a fortification.
l. 22. *Dipper:* a diving bird.
l. 23. *Elver:* a young eel.
P. 153, l. 6. *Spinney:* a copse.
l. 10. *Vole:* the water-rat.
l. 21. *Gorgons:* three sisters, one of whom, Medusa, by her fearful appearance, turned to stone everyone who looked at her.

Portrait of a Boy.
Stephen Vincent Benét, born at Bethlehem, Pennsylvania (1898), and a graduate of Yale University, comes of a family of army officers. "John Brown's Body" (1928) deals with the American Civil War.

P. 154, l. 13. (*Southern*) *Cross:* a constellation of the Southern hemisphere.
Mars: one of the planets.
l. 14. *Centaur:* a constellation.
l. 15. *Wattled:* with flesh under the throat, like a turkey.
l. 21. *Syenite:* a granular igneous rock.
l. 24. *Doubloons:* a Spanish gold coin, worth about a guinea.

Sir Hudibras and his Squire.
Samuel Butler (1612-1680) was a satirical poet of the Restoration, and his greatest poem, "Hudibras,"

NOTES TO THE POEMS

was an effective satire on the Puritans in the style of Don Quixote. By its mock-heroic effects, it is comparable, though at a distance, with " The Rape of the Lock," and by its satire with " Absalom and Achitophel."

P. 157, l. 1. *Dudgeon :* anger, a quarrel ; here, the Civil War, 1642-6.
ll. 5–6. *Gospel trumpeter, long-ear'd rout :* the Puritans.
Rout : company.
ll. 15–16. *Blow . . . shoulder-blade :* the accolade ; the light blow or touch on the shoulder with the flat of a drawn sword, with which the king or queen confers a knighthood. The knight was addressed as " Right worshipful."
l. 17. *Errant :* wandering.
l. 18. *Cartel :* a challenge.
Warrant : a document conferring certain powers, *e.g.* that of arresting a suspected person.
l. 19. *On the bench :* as a magistrate, in the Courts.
l. 20. *Bind o'er :* a legal term, meaning " to make an accused person promise to keep the peace, or to appear in the court on another day."
Swaddle : to wrap in bandages, as was formerly done with new-born children.
l. 22. *Styl'd of war . . . peace :* a soldier and a Justice of the Peace.
l. 23. *Amphibious :* able to live either on land or in water.
l. 28. *Pother :* fuss, turmoil.
l. 30. *Grain :* a very small unit of weight.
P. 158, l. 2. *Montaigne :* a great French writer of the sixteenth century. His *Essays*, the first of their kind, are notable for their tolerant and practical wisdom.
l. 16. *Trope :* a figure of speech.
l. 23. *Rhetorician :* orator.

The Character of Shaftesbury.

John Dryden (1631–1700). In an age when authors of no independent means depended largely on the patronage of the Court, Dryden was put to many political shifts to maintain his position. He began by writing verses in praise of Cromwell. With the Restoration (1660) he turned to drama, a taste for which Charles II had acquired during his exile in France. He wrote " heroic plays," and blank verse tragedies, of which his best is "All for Love." He was appointed Poet Laureate in 1670. He excelled in satiric poetry and found scope for his talent in the political controversies that arose round the Earl of Shaftesbury and the Duke of Monmouth's succession to the throne. He satirised Shaftesbury (in favour of Charles's brother, the Duke of York) in "Absalom and Achitophel" (1681). Perhaps with an eye to the future of politics (James was a Catholic), Dryden became a Catholic in the same year and wrote "The Hind and the Panther" defending the Church of Rome against the Church of England. Dryden's prose imported clearness and precision from France, and "An Essay of Dramatic Poesie" (1668), with the Prefaces to his poems, earned him the title of "The Father of English Prose."

Achitophel was the counsellor of Absalom, in his rebellion against his father David. *See* 2 Samuel xv-xvii.

In this poem David is Charles II, Absalom the Duke of Monmouth, and Achitophel the Earl of Shaftesbury. In the reign of Charles II, Shaftesbury and his followers, who were nicknamed Whigs, wished to exclude James (Charles's brother) from the succession, since he was an avowed Catholic. For this purpose they introduced, in 1679, the Exclusion Bill. Charles saved his brother by dissolving Parliament.

The Duke of Monmouth was proposed as successor to the throne by Shaftesbury and the Whigs, and on Charles's death he made an unsuccessful attempt to seize the throne, being defeated at Sedgemoor.

Epitaph on Charles II.

John Wilmot, Earl of Rochester (1647-1680), was one of the friends of Charles II and distinguished himself in the Dutch wars. For wit, versatility, and intellectual vitality he stands high above the level of the age.

The Combat (from *The Rape of the Lock*).

Alexander Pope (1688-1744) attained early to great perfection of rhythm and expression—he "lisp'd in numbers"—but his mind received an odd twist from the facts that he was practically a cripple and that he suffered certain disabilities through being a Catholic. He found fittest expression in satire. He excelled in the use of the heroic couplet, which he perfected as a

NOTES TO THE POEMS

satirical weapon in the mock-heroic "Rape of the Lock" (1712) and "The Dunciad" (1728). His "Essay on Criticism" (1711) and "Essay on Man" (1734) are clever re-statements of other men's ideas. Pope completed verse translations of Homer's "Iliad" (1720) and "Odyssey" (1726), which made his fortune. His poetry has a matchless glitter and, after Shakespeare, his poetic aphorisms are probably more often quoted than those of any other English poet.

P. 160, l. 15. *Pallas :* the Greek goddess of wisdom.
Mars : the Roman god of war.
Latona : daughter of the Titan Coeus and Phoebe, and mother of Apollo.
Hermes : Mercury, the herald and messenger of the gods.
l. 16. *Olympus :* a mountain in Greece, supposed to be the home of the gods.
l. 18. *Neptune :* the god of the sea.
P. 161, l. 1. *Maeander :* a river in Asia Minor.
P. 162, l. 5. *Othello :* the Shakespearean protagonist whose jealousy of Desdemona, his wife, was aggravated by seeing her handkerchief in the possession of another.
l. 13. *The Muse :* the goddess of poetry.
l. 16. *Proculus :* a Roman senator, to whom Romulus, after his death, is said to have appeared, and whom he informed that the Roman people were thereafter to honour him as a god.

Elegy on the Death of a Mad Dog.
P. 163, l. 5. *Islington :* now a district of London; formerly a village outside the city.
l. 18. *Pique :* ill-feeling, quarrel.

Fred.
P. 164, l. 5. *Fred :* Frederick, Prince of Wales, son of George II.
l. 13. *The whole generation :* the Hanoverians.

The Colubriad.
William Cowper (1731-1800), the son of a clergyman of Great Berkhampstead, was educated at Westminster School, and articled to the law. His serious, melancholy temper which turned at times into madness, appears in "The Castaway" and "On the Receipt of my Mother's Picture." Occasionally he turned for relief to lighter humorous themes, as in "John Gilpin." His quiet years of retirement are mirrored

POEMS OLD AND NEW

in poems on his various pets, " Epitaph on a Hare,"
" The Retired Cat," and in his chief poem, " The
Task." In order to divert his mind from melancholy
he undertook a blank verse translation of Homer.
His " Letters " are notable.

In a letter dated August 3, 1782, Cowper gives the
following prose account of this incident :—

" Passing from the greenhouse to the barn, I saw
three kittens . . . looking with fixed attention at something, which lay on the threshold of a door, coiled up.
I took but little notice of them at first ; but a loud
hiss engaged me to attend more closely, when behold
—a viper ! the largest I remember to have seen,
rearing itself, darting its forked tongue, and ejaculating
the aforementioned hiss at the nose of a kitten almost
in contact with his lips. I ran into the hall for a
hoe with a long handle, with which I intended to
assail him, and returning in a few seconds missed
him : he was gone, and I feared had escaped me.
Still, however, the kitten sat watching immoveably
upon the same spot. I concluded, therefore, that,
sliding between the door and the threshold, he had
found his way out of the garden into the yard. I
went round immediately, and there found him in
close conversation with the old cat, whose curiosity
being excited by so novel an appearance, inclined her
to pat his head repeatedly with her fore foot ; with her
claws, however, sheathed, and not in anger ; but in the
way of philosophical inquiry and examination. To
prevent her falling a victim to so laudable an exercise
of her talents, I interposed in a moment with the hoe,
and performed upon him an act of decapitation,
which though not immediately mortal, proved so in
the end."

Colubriad : a poetical narrative about a viper, as the
" Iliad " is the poetical narrative of Ilion, or Troy.

P. 165, l. 5. *Count de Grasse :* A French admiral who
defeated Howe in the West Indies during the War of
American Independence.

Queue : pigtail.

l. 29. *Phenomenon :* wonder.

The Jackdaw of Rheims.

Richard Harris Barham (1788–1845), born at Canterbury
and educated at St. Paul's School and Brasenose College,
Oxford, was ordained in 1813. His series of humor-

NOTES TO THE POEMS

ous poems, "The Ingoldsby Legends," half narrative, half parody, appeared mostly in the "Miscellany" begun in 1837 by his old schoolfellow Richard Bentley.

P. 166, l. 9. *Lord Primate*: the Cardinal Lord Archbishop.

l. 21. *Rochet*: a close-fitting linen vestment worn by bishops.

Pall: cloak, mantle.

l. 22. *Mitre*: a head-dress worn by bishops.

Crosier: the staff of a bishop.

P. 167, l. 7. *Flawn*: custard, pancake.

l. 9. *Stole*: a long robe reaching to the feet.

l. 12. *Refectory*: the place where meals are taken, especially in a monastery.

l. 14. *Emboss'd*: ornamented with raised work.

l. 15. *Rheims*: in N. France: famous for its cathedral.

Namur: in Belgium.

l. 19. *Eau de Cologne*: a perfumed spirit.

l. 24. *Diaper*: unbleached linen cloth woven in slightly defined figures.

l. 29. *Turquoise*: a precious stone, bluish green.

King Canute.

William Makepeace Thackeray (1811-1863), born in India, was sent at five to England and educated at Charterhouse and Cambridge. His first novel was "Barry Lyndon" (1842). "Vanity Fair" (1847) was his first great success. "The Newcomes," "Pendennis," and "Henry Esmond" are among his greatest works.

P. 173, l. 4. *The Jewish captain*: Joshua.

"Then spake Joshua to the Lord in the day when the Lord delivered up the Amorites before the children of Israel, and he said in the sight of Israel, Sun, stand thou still upon Gibeon; and thou, Moon, in the valley of Ajalon.

"And the sun stood still, and the moon stayed, until the people had avenged themselves upon their enemies."

—Joshua x. 12-13.

You are old, Father William.

Lewis Carroll (Charles Lutwidge Dodgson, 1832-1898) was a mathematical lecturer at Christ Church, Oxford, and wrote mathematical treatises. "Alice in Wonderland" (1865) and a number of similar fantasies are only another expression of his logical genius; in verbal logical absurdity he has probably never been surpassed.

POEMS OLD AND NEW

Waste.
 (Captain) Harry J. C. Graham (*b.* 1874) is a journalist, a trustee of the British Museum, and a prolific writer of sporting literature, light fiction, and humorous verse, of which "Ruthless Rhymes" is one of the most characteristic volumes.

Star Talk.
 Robert Ranke Graves (*b.* 1895) was educated at Oxford, and has issued several books of poetry and prose. His best work is the autobiography, "Good-bye to All That" (1929), which includes, like many of his poems, his reminiscences of the War.
 The *zodiac* is the belt of the heavens which the sun traverses during the year. It was anciently divided into twelve equal parts called the signs of the zodiac, which corresponded to twelve constellations: most of these went by the name of an animal (Greek—*zoon*), the shape of which the stars in that constellation resembled by their arrangement.
 The twelve signs were :—Aries (the Ram), Taurus (the Bull), Gemini (the Twins), Cancer (the Crab), Leo (the Lion), Virgo (the Virgin), Libra (the Balance), Scorpio (the Scorpion), Sagittarius (the Archer), Capricornus (the Goat), Aquarius (the Water-bearer), and Pisces (the Fishes).

P. 176, l. 1. *Gemelli :* Gemini, the Twins.
 l. 9. *Pleiads :* a group of seven stars in the shoulder of the constellation Taurus.
 l. 11. *Hyads :* a cluster of five stars in the constellation Taurus.
 l. 17. *Orion :* a hunter placed among the stars at his death. His figure is formed by seven very bright stars, three of which, in a straight line, form the hunter's belt (l. 21).
 l. 20. *The Great Bear :* a constellation.
 l. 22. *Pelt :* skin, hide.
P. 177, l. 5. *Venus :* the most brilliant of the planets.
 l. 6. *Mars :* a planet.

QUESTIONS ON THE POEMS

Sir Patrick Spens.
   1. This ballad is a condensed drama : divide it into scenes and expand into a short play. Where do gaps occur in the story ?
   2. What ballad devices are here used ?
   3. Compare this with any modern ballad. Which do you consider superior and for what reasons ?
   4. Quote two passages in the ballad that suggest that the author was a blunt, satirical fellow.
   5. Write a short ballad on (*a*) the wreck of the White Ship, (*b*) Alfred and the cakes, (*c*) Canute and the waves, (*d*) any similar incident, real or legendary.

Helen of Kirconnell.
   1. Expand the story as a connected narrative or as a short play.
   2. If you were setting this poem to music, what would be the chief qualities of your setting ?
   3. What is meant by " realism " in description ? Write a note on the realism of this ballad and of the old ballads generally.

Rosabelle.
   1. In what respects does this poem resemble an ancient ballad ?
   2. Scott relates several of the incidents indirectly. Point these out. Consider how far this method is necessary and effective.
   3. Does Scott introduce the supernatural element effectively ? Mention other poems in which the supernatural is introduced and compare them with " Rosabelle."
   4. Comment on Scott's use of (*a*) proper names, (*b*) vowel-music.

Proud Maisie.
   1. How does Scott emphasise the pride of Maisie ?
   2. Mention other ballads in which a bird speaks or acts

POEMS OLD AND NEW

like a human being. Does Scott succeed, in this poem, in making the device seem natural?

Bishop Hatto.
1. Point out any respect in which this poem seems far-fetched or unnatural.
2. Tell briefly any other story that would serve as the theme of a similar poem—a story in which animals carry out a just revenge.

La Belle Dame sans Merci.
1. How has Keats departed from the usual ballad stanza?
2. What features of the ballad does he retain?
3. Point out words and phrases by which he builds up an atmosphere of magic. Compare the poem and its effect with " The Listeners " by Walter de la Mare.
4. Name other poems that deal with supernatural events. How do they resemble or differ from this poem?
5. Quote phrases to show that Keats was a master of the horrible. Compare these with similar descriptions by any other poet.
6. Compare the first two stanzas with the description in the " Ode to Autumn " (p. 117).
7. Draw a picture of the " Belle Dame sans Merci."

The Knight's Leap.
1. What is the grim joke in the poem? What light does it throw on the knight's character? Is the knight a real hero?
2. How is the style of the poem in keeping with the character of the knight?
3. Write a short description of the life of knights in the Middle Ages, and of the manner of this knight in particular.

Horatius.
1. What is meant by " suspense " in a story? At what point in this poem is the suspense most acute? Is it handled effectively?
2. Write a paragraph describing Roman society as Macaulay pictures it.
3. Comment on Macaulay's similes. Are they effective?
4. Write an argument defending or attacking " The Brave Days of Old."

Shameful Death.
1. Does the poet's departure from the chronological order of events improve the narrative?

QUESTIONS ON THE POEMS

2. How does Morris create an open-air feeling in this poem?

3. Comment on the conclusion. Why does it differ in rhythm and style from the rest of this poem?

4. Point out any specially expressive words and phrases in this poem.

The Ballad of Semmerwater.

1. What contrast forms the central subject of this poem?
2. How does the poet invest the submerged city with an atmosphere of romance?
3. What ballad devices are used in the poem?
4. Comment on the use made of (*a*) long vowels, (*b*) alliteration, (*c*) repetition.
5. What kind of tune would best suit the poem?
6. Mention any other legends about the regions under the sea.

Hart-Leap Well.

1. Wordsworth says that his purpose was " to imitate, and, as far as possible, to adopt the very language of men." How far has Wordsworth succeeded in this poem in writing the ordinary speech of men?
2. " The moving accident is not my trade;
    To freeze the blood I have no ready arts:
    'Tis my delight, alone in summer shade,
    To pipe a simple song for thinking hearts."

From this, or any other narrative poem of Wordsworth's, illustrate this statement of his purpose.

3. Wordsworth draws his similes from Nature. Illustrate from this poem.
4. What is the moral of this poem? Compare it with the moral of " The Rime of the Ancient Mariner."

The Destruction of Sennacherib.

1. Point out details that emphasise (*a*) the greatness and wealth of the Assyrians, (*b*) the sudden and complete destruction that overtook them.
2. Comment on use of (*a*) simile, (*b*) antithesis.
3. Does the metre suit the subject of the poem?

The Armada.

1. Discuss the effectiveness of Macaulay's plan for showing how the alarm spread over England.
2. Do you think the use of proper names in this poem effective? Compare it with the use made of them by Scott

POEMS OLD AND NEW

in "Rosabelle." What might be said against Macaulay's introduction of so much geographical detail?

Morte d'Arthur.

1. Compare Tennyson's impression of the Age of Chivalry with that of Morris in "Shameful Death." Which do you think is nearer the truth? Compare also Sir Walter Scott's, as in "Ivanhoe."

2. Quote passages where onomatopoeia is used effectively.

3. Tennyson has been accused of straining after effect. Point out any expressions that might justify this charge by seeming forced or artificial.

4. Compare Tennyson's account with Malory's (p. 189). What has Tennyson added or altered?

The Lady of Shalott.

1. Point out passages where Tennyson uses a number of bright colours together. If you can, examine any of the pictures of Burne-Jones, Rossetti, or Morris, and notice the similarity: or compare with Rossetti's "The Blessed Damozel" or Morris's lyrics.

2. Contrast the atmosphere at the beginning of the poem with that at the end (§ 4). How is each built up?

3. Write a paragraph describing (*a*) the castle of Shalott, (*b*) the surrounding country.

4. Relate briefly any other story of a curse or a charm and the effect of breaking it.

5. Is the curse reasonable? How does Tennyson make us accept it?

6. Write a short appreciation of Tennyson's descriptions of landscape and people. Quote specially vivid phrases or passages.

Hervé Riel.

1. Write a note on the metre and rhyme of this poem.

2. Point out examples of abruptness of style and incomplete sentences. Do these obscure the meaning? What is their effect on the narration?

3. Contrast the deed and the reward.

4. "All in the day's work." Write a short story under this title.

The Pied Piper of Hamelin.

1. What devices does Browning use for humorous effect? Point out rhymes that produce humour.

2. Write a short appreciation of Browning's description of (*a*) the Piper, (*b*) the rats, (*c*) the children.

QUESTIONS ON THE POEMS

3. Quote from this poem to show that Browning was a lover of music. Mention other narratives or legends that illustrate the power of music.

4. Work out, in two columns, the parallel facts in the balance between the rats and the children.

5. Draw a picture of the Pied Piper with the children following him.

Goblin Market.

1. Write an appreciation of the descriptions. Refer to particular passages.

2. Mention other poems dealing with fairies or goblins and compare them with this poem.

3. Write a note on the similes of this poem and the metre.

A Runnable Stag.

1. Relate briefly the story told in this poem.

2. Mention any other English poems that describe a hunt. Are they more, or less, exciting than this? Can you account for the difference?

3. Write a note on the metre and its appropriateness to the subject.

4. How does the poet arouse our sympathy and admiration for the stag?

5. Quote expressions that seem to you specially poetical, vivid, or imaginative, and say why they appeal to you.

Hawke.

1. Draw a rough plan of Quiberon Bay, showing the direction of the wind and the positions of Hawke's and the French fleets at the beginning of the battle.

2. What pun adds to the effect of the poem? How is it sustained? What use is made of onomatopoeia to reinforce the pun?

He fell among Thieves.

1. Write out fully the narrative of the man who had fallen among thieves.

2. What is the source of the title?

3. Write a connected account of the hero's life in England.

4. Write a paragraph on the poet's descriptions of Nature. Point out specially effective words and phrases.

The Highwayman.

1. Compare the moonlight descriptions with those in (*a*) " Morte d'Arthur " (p. 40), and (*b*) " Hymn to Diana " (p. 101).

2. What use does the poet make of colour in Part I?
3. Point out figurative phrases that are specially vivid.
4. Where is the most exciting point in the story?
5. Mention any other poems dealing with similar adventures. Compare them with this poem.
6. Draw a picture of the Highwayman.

The Passionate Shepherd to his Love.
1. What is a "pastoral" poem? Is the pastoral convention justified? Compare its use in this poem with its use in "The Scholar Gipsy" (p. 121).
2. Is the shepherd's vision true to life?
3. Point out examples of alliteration, and of the use of musical language.

Winter.
1. What winter scenes does Shakespeare suggest?
2. Point out words denoting (a) movement, (b) inaction.
3. How does Shakespeare emphasise the impression of cold?
4. What information about country life in Shakespeare's day can be gathered from the poem?
5. Write a short description, preferably in verse, of a winter scene in town or village.

Fidele.
1. What is a dirge? Is this a good example? Compare it with "Soldier, rest!" (p. 107). What consolation has Shakespeare to offer in view of death?
2. From this poem illustrate Shakespeare's knowledge of (a) the Old Testament, (b) Aesop's "Fables."
3. Comment on the use of (a) metonymy, (b) pun. What is the finest epithet in the poem?

Character of a Happy Life.
1. Compare this ideal of a happy life with those outlined in "The Passionate Shepherd" (p. 97) and "Innisfree" (p. 137). How does this differ in character from the others?
2. Write a paragraph (or a short poem) describing your own ideal of a happy life.

To Celia.
1. What is a "conceit"? Point out one in this poem.
2. Rewrite the substance of this poem in prose.

QUESTIONS ON THE POEMS

Hymn to Diana.
1. Comment on the music of this poem.
2. Write an appreciation of the personification of the Moon.

The Village Preacher and *The Village Schoolmaster.*
1. Is Goldsmith's a fair or a flattering description of a typical schoolmaster? Compare his description with that of any other famous schoolmasters in fiction.
2. Compare the Preacher with Mr. Primrose in " The Vicar of Wakefield."
3. Write a note on the humour of these sketches. Compare them with " Jack " (p. 138).
4. Write a similar sketch of a modern preacher or schoolmaster.

The Tiger.
1. What points does Blake select for emphasis in the Tiger?
2. Follow out the simile of the smith and the anvil.
3. Write a paragraph on Blake's peculiarities of language and ideas.
4. Name a few other poems that describe animals. How do they differ in treatment from this poem?
5. Read Francis Thompson's poem " To a Snowflake," and compare the main idea with that of " The Tiger."

The Solitary Reaper.
1. How does Wordsworth emphasise the idea of loneliness?
2. Summarise briefly in prose the subject of this poem.
3. Quote lines or phrases in which Wordsworth seems to have captured " magic " of description and expression.

Westminster Bridge.
1. Compare Wordsworth's description with that of his sister (p. 197), in respect of (*a*) the picture drawn, (*b*) the language, (*c*) the idea.
2. Mention two or three other poems that deal with London. What aspects have they chosen?
3. Write an essay on the aspect of London that most appeals to you.
4. What is a sonnet? Attempt a sonnet on one of the following : (*a*) a landscape, (*b*) one of the seasons, (*c*) your favourite author, (*d*) the flight of time.

POEMS OLD AND NEW

She dwelt among the untrodden ways.
  1. Write a note on the simplicity of the idea and of the style of this poem. Does the poem gain or lose by it?
  2. Are the similes characteristic of Wordsworth?

Lullaby.
  1. What is a lullaby? Does this poem conform to the ordinary type of lullaby?
  2. Compare it in subject and style with any other lullabies you know, *e.g.* that sung by the fairies in " A Midsummer Night's Dream." How is the subject of this lullaby unusual?

Soldier, rest!
  1. How does this poem differ from others on similar subjects, *e.g.* " Fidele " (p. 98), " Coronach " (p. 109)?
  2. What do you gather from this poem about its author?
  3. Collect the words that describe sounds and remark on their appropriateness.

Coronach.
  1. What is a coronach?
  2. What information about Duncan can you gather from this poem?
  3. Point out and comment on the figures of speech which occur in the poem.
  4. What is the most memorable line in the poem?

Pibroch of Donuil Dhu.
  1. How does the metre suggest speed and the urgency of the summons? By what similes and details does Scott suggest this idea?
  2. Name some other poems where (*a*) similar metre, (*b*) similar devices, are used to produce a similar effect.
  3. Write a stanza in this style, similar in subject to the third.

Kubla Khan
  1. Describe with a diagram the course of the River Alph, and the position of the palace.
  2. In your own words, give briefly the general meaning of the last section (*A damsel* . . . end).
  3. How does Coleridge suggest (*a*) the richness, (*b*) the romance, (*c*) the savage aspect, of the scenery?
  4. Write a note on the metrical movement of the poem.
  5. Write a short note on Coleridge's powers of description and command of language as exemplified in this poem.

QUESTIONS ON THE POEMS

The Parrot.
 1. Quote details of the contrasts made between (*a*) Mull and America, (*b*) the parrot on its arrival and later.
 2. How is the bird treated by the poet as a human being?
 3. Tell any similar anecdote, preferably in verse, about a parrot or any other pet.

She walks in beauty.
 1. Whence does Byron draw the similes in this poem? To what poet's influence would you attribute this?
 2. Collect details that bring out the contrast.

To Night.
 1. Illustrate from this poem Shelley's (*a*) love of Nature, (*b*) abstract description.
 2. Write a note on Shelley's use of personification.
 3. Comment on Shelley's vowel-music and his use of liquid-consonants (*l, m, n, r,*), the movement of his verse, and his use of alliteration and figures of speech.
 4. "Shelley's proper sphere was music." Does this poem bear out the criticism?
 5. Compare this poem with a poem by Scott or Byron. What quality do you find lacking in Shelley or in the other poet you have compared with him?

The Human Seasons.
 1. Comment on the form of this sonnet. Compare its form with that of the following sonnet (p. 116).
 2. Which season did Keats favour? Contrast the view of autumn given here with those given in "Autumn" (p. 117) and in "La Belle Dame sans Merci." (p. 12).
 3. What famous passage in Shakespeare deals with the same subject—the stages of man's life? Compare and contrast the two.

On first Looking into Chapman's Homer.
 1. What is the most effective phrase in the poem?
 2. Write a short appreciation of the two similes used in the sonnet.
 3. Write a paragraph on the book or poem that has most affected you in a similar way.

Autumn.
 1. Does Keats give a full and true picture of autumn? Compare his description with that given in (*a*) Clare's

POEMS OLD AND NEW

"Autumn," (*b*) the first stanza of Shelley's "Ode to the West Wind."

2. From this poem give examples of Keats's delight in richness of (*a*) sound, (*b*) colour, (*c*) taste.

3. Comment on the use of personification in the second stanza of this poem.

Autumn.

1. Contrast the aspects of autumn described by Clare and Keats.

2. Write a paragraph on Clare's descriptions of Nature.

3. Write a note on the language of this poem, and quote expressive phrases.

4. Using as a basis the details given by Keats and Clare, write a description of autumn in the country, or describe an autumn country scene based on your own observation during one of your walks.

5. Paint a picture of an autumn landscape.

The Eagle.

1. Write a note on the use, in this poem, of (*a*) simile, (*b*) onomatopoeia, (*c*) expressive verbs and adjectives.

2. How does Tennyson here give the impression of space?

Blow, Bugle, blow.

1. Write a note on the glamour of this poem. How is it achieved?

2. Work out the contrast between the echoes of Nature and of the Soul.

3. How is the impression of distance created by the poet?

4. Write a short moonlight description in the same style. (Cp. "The Merchant of Venice," "How sweet the moonlight . . .").

Home-Thoughts, from Abroad.

1. By what details does Browning suggest the freshness of England in spring?

2. Quote from the poem to show that Browning was fond of (*a*) flowers, (*b*) birds, (*c*) music.

3. Compare the appreciation of England with Yeats's appreciation of Ireland (p. 137).

O Captain! My Captain!

1. Write a note on the metaphor of the ship of state.

2. Criticise the rhymes. Write a note on the stanza scheme.

QUESTIONS ON THE POEMS

The Scholar Gipsy.
 1. When Arnold wrote this poem he was still comparatively young. What light does the poem throw on his state of mind at that time?
 2. It has been said that Arnold and his friends lived at Oxford as in a great country house. How does this poem confirm that statement?
 3. Arnold speaks of poetry having "natural magic." Point out adjectives and phrases in which he achieves this magic in his own descriptions of Nature.
 4. Compare the stanza-form with that used in Keats's "Ode to a Nightingale" or "Autumn" (p. 117).

Itylus.
 1. Comment on the vowel-music and poetical devices (*e.g.* alliteration) in this poem. Do they injure the sense?
 2. Write a note on the rhymes and stanza-form.
 3. Mention other English poems on the nightingale. What do they say, and what does Swinburne here say, about the bird?

Pied Beauty.
 1. Comment on (*a*) the metre, (*b*) the language, (*c*) the power of description, in this poem.
 2. Compare this with other "catalogue" poems, *e.g.* R. Brooke's "Great Lover" and "The Dead" (p. 152).

A Passer-By.
 1. Are the poet's descriptions drawn from intimate knowledge or are they only conventional?
 2. Quote words and expressions by which Bridges emphasises (*a*) the dignity, (*b*) the "tidiness," of the ship.
 3. Mention other poems describing a sailing-ship and compare with this.
 4. Write a note on the metre and stanza-form of this poem.

The Vagabond.
 1. Mention any other poems of the open road, and compare their ideal of life with Stevenson's. Do you think Stevenson's account adequate or formed from experience?
 2. Quote any specially effective expressions.

Romance.
 1. Compare this poem with "The Passionate Shepherd to his Love" (p. 97). Contrast the inducements of the two lovers.

POEMS OLD AND NEW

2. How does this poem illustrate Stevenson's love of open-air life and wide spaces?

Drake's Drum.

1. What information can you gather about Drake from this poem alone?
2. Point out expressions that are specially appropriate in the mouth of a sailor.
3. Write a short note on (*a*) the use of dialect, (*b*) the refrain, (*c*) the metre.
4. Mention other poems on Drake and the Armada.
5. Write a parody of the poem.

The Hawk.

1. This poem shows "Nature, red in tooth and claw." Compare this view of Nature with Wordsworth's. How far is each true?
2. Write a short appreciation of the poet's description of (*a*) the atmosphere of the moors, (*b*) the terror of the bird.

The Lake Isle of Innisfree.

1. Write a paragraph bringing out the contrast of the city and the country stated in this poem.
2. Comment on the poet's use of words expressing, (*a*) sound, (*b*) colour. How does he suggest (*a*) the beauty of water, (*b*) peace? How far are his effects assisted by the use of repetition, onomatopoeia, and alliteration?
3. Compare this as a poem of the simple life with Wotton's "Character of a Happy Life" (p. 99) and Rogers's poem "A Wish" (Golden Treasury).
4. There is a legend that this poem was composed by the poet while he was standing on an island in Charing Cross while attempting to cross the street blocked with traffic. Comment.

The Scholars.

1. Is this a fair estimate of the scholar's life and work?
2. Read Southey's poem, "The Scholar," and Browning's "The Grammarian's Funeral," and contrast the views of these two poets with the view of Yeats.
3. Write a paragraph expressing your own view of the scholar's life.

Jack.

1. How is Jack's character reflected in the attitude towards him of (*a*) his wife, (*b*) the village children, (*c*) the doctor, (*d*) the parson, (*e*) the schoolmaster, (*f*) the head-keeper?

QUESTIONS ON THE POEMS

2. What (*a*) good qualities, (*b*) weaknesses, make Jack a lovable character? What is to be said in defence of his way of life?

3. Write a paragraph on E. V. Lucas as a humorist. Compare him with Goldsmith (p. 101).

4. Write a similar sketch, either in prose or in verse, of a village worthy you have known.

The Changeling.

1. Compare the fairies in this poem with the goblins in "Goblin Market" (p. 67).

2. Write a note on the descriptions of Nature in the fourth stanza.

3. Comment on the attitude of (*a*) the child to its parents, (*b*) the parents to the child. What justifies the application to the child of the name "changeling"?

4. Write a short note on (*a*) the stanza-form, (*b*) poetical devices used in this poem, *e.g.* alliteration, middle rhyme.

Stupidity Street.

1. How does the poet emphasise his astonishment and disgust?

2. Express in a sentence the moral of this poem. Compare it with the argument put forward in "Tit for Tat" (p. 146).

Roundabouts and Swings.

1. What information about gipsies can you get from this poem?

2. The gipsy is evidently contented. Compare his ideal of a happy life with the ideals of *e.g.* Wotton (p. 99), "The Vagabond" (p. 134), or "Innisfree" (p. 137).

3. Write a short essay from experience or imagination, describing life in a caravan.

4. Mention any other poem or book dealing with the gipsy life. Compare the gipsies there with this one.

5. Write a short paragraph describing the scene of the meeting in the lane.

6. Draw a picture of gipsies.

Tit for Tat.

1. What is the poet's argument against cruelty to animals? Is it a good one? Compare it with the arguments used in Wordsworth's "Hart-Leap Well" (p. 29) and Coleridge's "The Rime of the Ancient Mariner."

2. Using the arguments given in this poem and in

POEMS OLD AND NEW

"Stupidity Street" (p. 144) and adding others of your own if possible, write a short statement of the case against cruelty to animals.

I met at eve.

1. Is this an effective personification of sleep? Mention others in English poetry: compare and contrast them with this.
2. Does this poem include all that might be said of Sleep? What aspects are omitted?
3. How does the sound of the poem increase the main impression of quiet and restfulness?

The Donkey.

1. Point out any phrases or passages where the language seems exaggerated or strained. Is the exaggeration justified?
2. Explain "walking parody on all four-footed things," " of ancient crooked will," and " I had my hour."
3. Write a poem on Balaam's Ass.

Cargoes.

1. Compare the descriptions of (a) the movement, (b) the cargoes, of the three ships.
2. Which ship has the poet's preference?
3. Write a note on the use of consonants to assist the sense.
4. Write a paragraph on Masefield as a poet of the sea.

Prometheus.

1. Do you think that the introduction of Prometheus is fitting in this poem about a match-seller?

The Ship.

1. What impression does the poet wish to convey? How does the metre reinforce this impression? Show how all the details of description are appropriate.
2. Write an account of what you think these sailors had accomplished.

The Old Ships.

1. Describe the appearance and cargo of the old ships the poet saw beyond Tyre. How is their present contrasted with their past condition?
2. Write a paragraph describing fully the older ship as the poet saw it. Quote words or phrases to show how old it was.

QUESTIONS ON THE POEMS

3. Comment on (a) Flecker's use of compound adjectives, (b) the metre of the poem.

4. Read the story of Ulysses in Lamb's "Adventures of Ulysses" or in Butcher and Lang's translation of the "Odyssey." Is Flecker's version of the origin of Ulysses' wanderings in keeping with the character of Ulysses?

Everyone Sang.

1. What state of feeling does the poet describe? What occasion may have suggested the subject to him?

2. Comment on the rhythm.

The Dead.

1. Is Brooke realistic or idealistic in his account of the ...?

2. Point out any particularly happy phrases in the poem.

3. Write a note on the parallel used in the last six lines.

The Pike.

1. Write an appreciation of the descriptions in this poem. Quote specially vivid metaphors and expressions.

2. How does the poet create an atmosphere of quietness, coolness, and greenness? What does he contrast with it?

Portrait of a Boy.

1. Contrast this portrait and its method with those given in "Jack" (p. 138), and "The Village Preacher" and "The Village Schoolmaster" (pp. 101-104).

2. Is this a characteristic portrait of a boy?

3. Illustrate from the second section the poet's sense of colour and sound.

4. Comment on the use of simile and metaphor in the poem.

Sir Hudibras and his Squire.

1. What is meant by irony? Point out the various examples used in the description of Sir Hudibras.

2. Write a note on Butler's use of rhyme.

3. This poem is a satire on the Puritans or Roundheads. What Puritan qualities are criticised in Sir Hudibras? In what other literary works have the Puritans been satirised?

4. Explain the word satire.

The Character of Shaftesbury.

1. What adjective or phrase in this extract would sum up Dryden's idea of Shaftesbury?

2. Point out and remark on the force and appropriateness of the several metaphors used by Dryden.
3. Write a note on the epigrammatic quality of Dryden's verse.
4. What is an allegory? Mention other famous allegories in English.
5. Mention other examples of "Great wits ... to madness near allied." How did this description apply to Shaftesbury?

Epitaph on Charles II.
1. Basing your poem on a similar paradoxical remark about some famous historical (or fictitious) character (*e.g.* James I—the wisest fool in Christendom), write his epitaph in the style of that on Charles II.

The Combat.
1. What is meant by calling a poem "mock-heroic"? Show how this poem deserves the name, *e.g.* how it preserves the heroic pretence and how it introduces the "mock" element. Name other mock-heroic poems in English.
2. Express in your own words what precisely happened in this extract.
3. It was said of Pope that "he turned Pegasus into a rocking-horse": from an examination of this extract, would you agree or disagree? Illustrate your answer from particular couplets.

On a Certain Lady at Court.
1. What is meant by the "point" of a story or description? Where should it be placed for effect? Does this poem lead up to and place it effectively?
2. In what way is this poem a satire on woman?

Elegy on the Death of a Mad Dog.
1. What is an elegy? How far does this poem agree with the definition?
2. What device does Goldsmith use throughout with humorous effect? Point out all the examples of its use.
3. What was the "wonder," and what does it imply?

Fred (*p.* 164), *The Desired Swan-Song* (*p.* 166), and *Was* (*p.* 175).
1. What is an epigram? Which of these epigrams seem to you most (*a*) humorous, (*b*) sarcastic? Compare the different methods by which they achieve their purpose.

QUESTIONS ON THE POEMS

2. Make an epigram in verse or prose on the subject of motor cars or the wireless.

The Colubriad.

1. By what tricks of style and language does Cowper turn this serious narrative into a humorous one? In what lines does he adopt the mock-heroic tone?

The Jackdaw of Rheims.

1. How is a humorous effect produced in this poem by (*a*) repetition, (*b*) accumulation of petty detail, (*c*) slang, (*d*) exaggeration? Is the poem as a whole humorous?

2. Draw a picture of the Jackdaw of Rheims in one of his exploits.

King Canute.

1. What is a caricature? How is this poem a caricature of (*a*) the King's conceit, (*b*) the flattery of the courtiers? How is it faithful to historical truth?

2. Point out passages where humour is the result of placing side by side the lofty and the trivial.

3. Draw a caricature of King Canute.

You are old, Father William.

1. What is the wittiest passage in this poem? Which of the jokes are rather boyish and obvious? At what points does the poet produce humour from circumstances that are totally improbable?

Star Talk.

1. Write a paragraph in appreciation of the personifications on which this poem is based.

2. What touches of human feeling and what trivial details make up the humorous effect?

3. Write a humorous poem on Moonshine Talk.

Printed in Great Britain by R. & R. CLARK, LIMITED, *Edinburgh.*

THE SCHOLAR'S LIBRARY

Fcap. 8vo.   *2s. 6d. each.*

NORTHANGER ABBEY. By JANE AUSTEN. Edited by Mrs. FREDERICK BOAS. Illustrated by HUGH THOMSON.

DR. JOHNSON: A Selection from Boswell's Biography. Edited by M. ALDERTON PINK, M.A.

A TALE OF TWO CITIES. By CHARLES DICKENS. With an Introduction by G. K. CHESTERTON, and Notes by GUY BOAS, M.A. Illustrated.

SYBIL, OR THE TWO NATIONS. By BENJAMIN DISRAELI. Edited by VICTOR COHEN. Illustrated by F. PEGRAM.

FAR FROM THE MADDING CROWD. By THOMAS HARDY. Edited by CYRIL ALDRED.

THE MAYOR OF CASTERBRIDGE. By THOMAS HARDY. Edited by Prof. VIVIAN DE SOLA PINTO.

THE RETURN OF THE NATIVE. By THOMAS HARDY. Edited by CYRIL ALDRED. With an Introduction by SYLVIA LYND.

STORIES AND POEMS OF THOMAS HARDY. Selected and Edited by N. V. MEERES, B.A.

UNDER THE GREENWOOD TREE. By Thomas Hardy. Edited by Adrian Alington.

THE WOODLANDERS. By Thomas Hardy. Edited by Cyril Aldred.

THE ILIAD AND THE ODYSSEY: Extracts from the Translations by Lang, Leaf and Myers, and Butcher and Lang. Edited by H. M. King and H. Spooner.

EOTHEN. By A. W. Kinglake. Edited by Guy Boas, M.A.

PARADISE LOST. Books I. and II. By John Milton. Edited by G. C. Irwin, M.A., B.L.S. With an Introduction by Guy Boas, M.A.

MODERN ENGLISH PROSE. Selected and Edited by Guy Boas, M.A.

MODERN POETRY 1922-1934: An Anthology. Selected and Edited by Maurice Wollman, M.A.

THE DIARY OF SAMUEL PEPYS: SELECTIONS. Edited by N. V. Meeres, B.A.

POEMS FOR YOUTH. Selected and Edited by A. S. Cairncross, M.A., D.Litt.

POEMS OLD AND NEW: An Anthology. Selected and Edited by A. S. Cairncross, M.A., D.Litt.

LONGER POEMS OLD AND NEW. Selected and Edited by A. S. CAIRNCROSS, M.A., D.Litt.

A "PUNCH" ANTHOLOGY. Selected and Edited by GUY BOAS, M.A.

AN ANTHOLOGY OF WIT. Selected and Edited by GUY BOAS, M.A.

READINGS FROM THE SCIENTISTS. Selected and Edited by EDWARD MASON, M.A., M.Ed.

SHORT MODERN PLAYS. Selected and Edited by GUY BOAS, M.A.

KIDNAPPED. By ROBERT LOUIS STEVENSON. Edited by JAN STRUTHER. Illustrated by C. E. BROCK, R.I.

TREASURE ISLAND. By ROBERT LOUIS STEVENSON. Edited by Mrs FREDERICK BOAS. Illustrated by H. M. BROCK, R.I.

"THE TIMES": AN ANTHOLOGY. Selected and Edited by M. ALDERTON PINK, M.A.

Shakespeare

ANTONY AND CLEOPATRA. Edited by GUY BOAS, M.A.

AS YOU LIKE IT. Edited by CICELY BOAS.

CORIOLANUS. Edited by Prof. VIVIAN DE SOLA PINTO.

CYMBELINE. Edited by GUY BOAS, M.A.

HAMLET. Edited by ADRIAN ALINGTON.

HENRY IV. Parts I. and II. Edited by M. ALDERTON PINK, M.A.

HENRY V. Edited by DOROTHY MARGARET STUART and E. V. DAVENPORT.

JULIUS CÆSAR. Edited by F. ALLEN, M.A.

KING LEAR. Edited by F. E. BUDD, B.A., Ph.D.

MACBETH. Edited by M. ALDERTON PINK, M.A.

THE MERCHANT OF VENICE. Edited by P. H. B. LYON, M.A.

A MIDSUMMER-NIGHT'S DREAM. Edited by CYRIL ALDRED. With an Introduction by WALTER DE LA MARE.

MUCH ADO ABOUT NOTHING. Edited by F. E. BUDD, B.A., Ph.D.

OTHELLO. Edited by GUY BOAS, M.A.

RICHARD II. Edited by LIONEL ALDRED. With an Introduction by ST. JOHN ERVINE.

RICHARD III. Edited by LIONEL ALDRED.

ROMEO AND JULIET. Edited by GUY BOAS, M.A.

THE TEMPEST. Edited by EDWARD THOMPSON, M.A., Ph.D.

TWELFTH NIGHT. Edited by N. V. MEERES, B.A.

THE WINTER'S TALE. Edited by GUY BOAS, M.A.

MACMILLAN AND CO. LTD., LONDON